1

Printed in the United States of America

Table of Contents

Introduction

Congratulations on continuing your education as you continue to prepare for becoming an educator! Before we get into the test content, we're sure you have questions – everybody does. "How hard is the exam?" "Can I pass on my first try?" "What if I don't? Can I take it again?" "What is even *on* the test?"

Don't worry! We have the answers to all of these questions and more.

While the exam isn't easy, proper planning and preparation can help ensure your success. Sure, you can take the exam again if you fail; but our goal is to give you the keys to outsmarting the exam – the first time around. These first few pages will detail everything you'll need to know about the exam, before leading you into the review material. So get ready to take some notes. Pace yourself. And above all, remember that you are taking the right first step in furthering your career.

Registering for the Exam

This can be done via telephone or computer.

> **By Phone**: Phone registration is only available in "emergency" situations, and is not applicable for "regular" or "late" registrations. Regular and Late registrations must be done by computer.

> **By Computer**: Available 24 hours a day and 7 days a week, simply visit www.in.nesinc.com and find your way to "internet registration" tab. Please note that registrations must be completed by 5:00pm to count for that day. Follow the step-by-step instructions to register, make necessary payment, and confirmation of your registration.

Testing Fees

Even if no additional fees are assessed, knowing that you'll be paying a lot your hard-earned money is an additional incentive to do your best on the exam. Re-taking the test will require you to pay the same fees again – not properly preparing can have expensive consequences!

- The test fee is $38 per subtest, but please note that test centers may at their discretion charge additional fees, so you must check beforehand!

What's on the Exam

The content of the question will follow the below categories

- <u>**Reading Comprehension**</u>
- <u>**Language Arts**</u>
- <u>**Mathematics**</u>

How is the Exam Scored?

You will be scored on a range of 100 to 300 points, with a passing score being 240 or greater.

Test Day

Identification Policy: You must bring to the test administration a current, government-issued identification printed in English, in the name in which you registered, bearing your photograph and signature. Copies will not be accepted.

Acceptable forms of government-issued identification include the following:

- Driver's license with photograph and signature
- Passport with photograph and signature
- State identification with photograph and signature (provided by the Department of Licensing for individuals who do not have a driver's license)
- National identification with photograph and signature
- Military identification with photograph and signature
- Alien Registration Card (green card, permanent resident visa)

Unacceptable forms of identification:

- draft classification cards
- credit cards of any kind
- social security cards, student IDs
- international driver's licenses
- international student IDs
- notary-prepared letters or documents
- employee identification cards
- learner's permits or any temporary identification cards
- automated teller machine (ATM) cards

If you do not have proper identification at the time of your test, you will be denied admission to the test session. If you are refused admission to the test for any reason, you will be considered absent and will receive no credit or refund of any kind.

If the name on your identification differs from the name in which you are registered, you must bring **official, original** verification of the change (e.g., original marriage certificate, original court order).

If you have any questions about your identification, call Evaluation Systems at (916) 928-4192 or (800) 784-4999 before the day of the test.

You MUST Bring

As you head to the testing center, don't forget to bring your ID and any necessary documentation, as well as your Admission Ticket.

You May NOT Bring

Basically, if it's not your Admission Ticket, ID, or any approved device, you can't have it with you. Specifically, you can't bring these items into the testing room:

1. Cell phones, smartphones, or PDAs.
2. Any electronic recording, photographic, or listening device.
3. Food, drink, or tobacco products.
4. Personal items (purses, backpacks, etc.).
5. Paper, pencils, notes, reference material, etc.
6. Weapons of any type.

As if those precautions were not enough, you can also expect to be fingerprinted and/or photographed after entering the testing facility. You may be asked to undergo a quick scan from a metal detecting device before being allowed into the testing room. Additionally, you may be asked to sign a waiver stating that you understand the test administration will be videotaped.

In the event that you object to any of these security measures, you will not be allowed to test.

After the Test

Your test scores will be reported to you, as well as the institution(s) listed when you registered. Check your "test dates" calendar online to see when score reports will be available.

Scores are sometimes delayed if there is a problem with the processing or if there is a new computer test being administered. In addition, your scores will be delayed if there are problems with your payment, and your scores may be permanently voided if you have any outstanding balance owed by you to Evaluation Systems after a test administration for which you were registered.

Unofficial Test Results at a Computer-Based Test Center

At the end of your test, you'll get an "unofficial score". Keep in mind that these scores are not valid for reporting as an official score. You will get your official recorded score at a later date that is valid for use in official capacities.

Chapter 1: Mathematics

The CASA Math section will test your knowledge of the following concepts:

- **Numbers and Operations**

- **Algebra**

- **Geometry**

- **Data Analysis**

- **Statistics**

- **Probability**

We'll provide an extensive review of these subjects, as well as giving you the chance to run some practice drills. However, this section is NOT designed to TEACH you math; the CASA covers math concepts learned through the tenth grade, which means you don't need to learn any new information. In fact, you don't need to worry at all about working with endless, bulky calculations; writing geometry proofs; working with imaginary numbers; Calculus; or Trigonometry – none of them are covered on the CASA.

Calculators

Even though you are allowed to use a calculator, don't rely on it. Actually, the less you use a calculator, the better. If you find yourself needing to plug in a large amount of numbers, then the chances are that you've missed a part of the problem. Write out your work – that makes it much easier to catch mistakes. Use your brain for the reasoning, and use the calculator to *check* your work!

The Most Common Mistakes

People make mistakes all the time – but during a test, those mistakes can make the difference between an excellent score, or one which falls below the requirements. Watch out for these common mistakes that people make on the CASA:

- Answering with the wrong sign (positive / negative).

- Mixing up the Order of Operations.

- Misplacing a decimal.

- Not reading the question thoroughly (and therefore providing an answer that was not asked for.)

- Circling the wrong letter, or filling in wrong circle choice.

If you're thinking, "Those are just common sense" – exactly! Most of the mistakes made on the CASA are simple mistakes. Regardless, they still result in a wrong answer and the loss of a potential point.

Strategies for the Mathematics Section

1. **Go Back to the Basics**: First and foremost, practice your basic skills: sign changes, order of operations, simplifying fractions, and equation manipulation. These are the skills used most on the CASA, though they are applied in different contexts. Remember that when it comes right down to it, all math problems rely on the four basic skills of addition, subtraction, multiplication, and division. All that changes is the order in which they are used to solve a problem.

2. **Don't Rely on Mental Math**: Using mental math is great for eliminating answer choices, but ALWAYS WRITE IT DOWN! This cannot be stressed enough. Use whatever paper is provided; by writing and/or drawing out the problem, you are more likely to catch any mistakes. The act of writing things down forces you to organize your calculations, leading to an improvement in your CASA score.

3. **The Three-Times Rule**:

   - **Step One – Read the question**: Write out the given information.

   - **Step Two – Read the question**: Set up your equation(s) and solve.

   - **Step Three – Read the question:** Make sure that your answer makes sense (is the amount too large or small, is the answer in the correct unit of measure, etc.).

4. **Make an Educated Guess**: Eliminate those answer choices which you are relatively sure are incorrect, and then guess from the remaining choices. Educated guessing is critical to increasing your score.

Math Concepts Tested on the CASA

You need to practice in order to score well on the test. To make the most out of your practice, use this guide to determine the areas for which you need more review. Most importantly, practice all areas under testing circumstances (a quiet area, a timed practice test, no looking up facts as you practice, etc.)

When reviewing, take your time and let your brain recall the necessary math. If you are taking the CASA, then you have already had course instruction in these areas. The examples given will "jog" your memory.

The next few pages will cover various math subjects (starting with the basics, but in no particular order), along with worked examples.

CASA Formulas and Facts (Given)

You might see the formulas provided, but you should still review them now, since they will not be given with descriptions or examples.

1. **Diameter of a Circle** = 2 * Radius (r).

2. **Circumference of a Circle** = 2 * Radius (r) * π.

3. **Area of a Circle** = π * Radius $(r)^2$.

4. **Area of a Rectangle** = Length (l) * Width (w).

5. **Area of a Triangle** = ½ * Base (b) * Height (h).

6. **Volume of a Cube** = Length (l) * Width (w) * Height (h).

7. **Volume of a Cylinder** = Height (h) * Radius $(r)^2$ * π.

8. **The Pythagorean Theorem** (Finding Diagonal Length): Length of the Diagonal $(c)^2$ = Sum of the Two Remaining Squared Sides ($a^2 + b^2$).

9. **Surface Area of a Sphere** = 4 * Radius $(r)^2$ * π.

10. **Volume of a Sphere** = $^4/_3$ * Radius $(r)^3$ * π.

11. **Number of Degrees of an Arc in a Circle** = 360°

12. **Measure of Degrees of a Straight Angle** = 180°.

13. **Sum of Degrees of the Angles in a Triangle** = 180°.

The next few pages will cover those formulas and facts which will not be given to you before the test. Review them thoroughly, and take advantage of the "Test Your Knowledge" sections that we've provided – practice makes perfect!

Formulas and Facts (NOT Given)

Positive & Negative Number Rules

(+) + (-) = Subtract the two numbers. Solution gets the sign of the larger number.

(-) + (-) = Negative number.

(-) * (-) = Positive number.

(-) * (+) = Negative number.

(-) / (-) = Positive number.

(-) / (+) = Negative number.

Order of Operations

PEMDAS – **P**arentheses/**E**xponents/**M**ultiply/**D**ivide/**A**dd/**S**ubtract

Perform the operations within parentheses first, and then any exponents. After those steps, perform all multiplication and division. (These are done from left to right, as they appear in the problem) Finally, do all required addition and subtraction, also from left to right as they appear in the problem.

Examples:

1. Solve $(-(2)^2 - (4 + 7))$:
   - $(-4 - 11) = -15$.

2. Solve $((5)^2 \div 5 + 4 * 2)$:
   - $25 \div 5 + 4 * 2$.
   - $5 + 8 = 13$.

✓ Greatest Common Factor (GCF)

The greatest factor that divides two numbers.

Example: The GCF of 24 and 18 is 6. 6 is the largest number, or greatest factor, that can divide both 24 and 18.

Probabilities

A probability is found by dividing the number of desired outcomes by the number of possible outcomes. (The piece divided by the whole.)

Example: What is the probability of picking a blue marble if 3 of the 15 marbles are blue?

3/15 = 1/5. The probability is **1 in 5** that a blue marble is picked.

Fractions

Adding and subtracting fractions requires a common denominator.

Find a common denominator for:

$$\frac{2}{3} - \frac{1}{5}.$$

$$\frac{2}{3} - \frac{1}{5} = \frac{2}{3}\left(\frac{5}{5}\right) - \frac{1}{5}\left(\frac{3}{3}\right) = \frac{10}{15} - \frac{3}{15} = \frac{7}{15}.$$

To add mixed fractions, work first the whole numbers, and then the fractions.

$$2\frac{1}{4} + 1\frac{3}{4} = 3\frac{4}{4} = 4.$$

To subtract mixed fractions, convert to single fractions by multiplying the whole number by the denominator and adding the numerator. Then work as above.

$$2\frac{1}{4} - 1\frac{3}{4} = \frac{9}{4} - \frac{7}{4} = \frac{2}{4} = \frac{1}{2}.$$

To multiply fractions, convert any mixed fractions into single fractions and multiply across; reduce to lowest terms if needed.

$$2\frac{1}{4} * 1\frac{3}{4} = \frac{9}{4} * \frac{7}{4} = \frac{63}{16} - 3\frac{15}{16}.$$

To divide fractions, convert any mixed fractions into single fractions, flip the second fraction, and then multiply across.

$$2\frac{1}{4} \div 1\frac{3}{4} = \frac{9}{4} \div \frac{7}{4} = \frac{9}{4} * \frac{4}{7} = \frac{36}{28} = 1\frac{8}{28} = 1\frac{2}{7}.$$

✓ Simple Interest

Interest * Principle.

Example: If I deposit $500 into an account with an annual rate of 5%, how much will I have after 2 years?

1st year: 500 + (500*.05) = 525.

2nd year: 525 + (525*.05) = **551.25**.

✓ Prime Factorization

Expand to prime number factors.

Example: 104 = 2 * 2 * 2 * 13.

Absolute Value

The absolute value of a number is its distance from zero, not its value.

So in $|x| = a$, "x" will equal "$-a$" as well as "a."

Likewise, $|3| = 3$, and $|-3| = 3$.

Equations with absolute values will have two answers. Solve each absolute value possibility separately. All solutions must be checked into the original equation.

Example: Solve for x: $|2x - 3| = x + 1$

1. Equation One: $2x - 3 = -(x + 1)$.
   - $2x - 3 = -x - 1$.
   - $3x = 2$.
   - $x = 2/3$.

2. Equation Two: $2x - 3 = x + 1$.
   - $x = 4$.

✓ Mean, Median, Mode

Mean is a math term for "average." Total all terms and divide by the number of terms.

Find the mean of 24, 27, and 18.

$24 + 27 + 18 = 69 \div 3 = \mathbf{23}$.

Median is the middle number of a given set, found after the numbers have all been put in numerical order. In the case of a set of even numbers, the middle two numbers are averaged.

What is the median of 24, 27, and 18?

18, **24**, 27.

What is the median of 24, 27, 18, and 19?

18, 19, 24, 27 ($19 + 24 = 43$. $43/2 = \mathbf{21.5}$).

Mode is the number which occurs most frequently within a given set.

What is the mode of 2, 5, 4, 4, 3, 2, 8, 9, 2, 7, 2, and 2?

The mode would be **2** because it appears the most within the set.

Combined Average

Weigh each average individual average before determining the sum.

> **Example**: If Cory averaged 3 hits per game during the summer and 2 hits per game during the fall and played 7 games in the summer and 8 games in the fall, what was his hit average overall?
>
> 1. Weigh each average.
>   - Summer: 3 * 7 = 21.
>   - Fall: 2 * 8 = 16.
>   - Sum: 21 + 16 = 47.
>
> 2. Total number of games: 7 + 8 = 15.
>
> 3. Calculate average: 47/15 = ~ **3.13 hits/game**.

You may need to work a combined average problem with a missing term.

> **Example**: Bobbie paid an average of $20 a piece for ten shirts. If five of the shirts averaged $15 each, what was the average cost of the remaining shirts?
>
> 1. Calculate sum: 10 * 20 = 200.
>
> 2. Calculate sub-sum #1: 5 *15 = 75.
>
> 3. Calculate sub-sum #2: 200 – 75 − 125.
>
> 4. Calculate average: 125 / 5 = **$25**.

Percent, Part, & Whole

Part = Percent * Whole.

Percent = Part / Whole.

Whole = Part / Percent.

> **Example:** Jim spent 30% of his paycheck at the fair. He spent $15 for a hat, $30 for a shirt, and $20 playing games. How much was his check? (Round to nearest dollar.)
>
> Whole = 65 / .30 = **$217.00**.

Percent Change

Percent Change = Amount of Change / Original Amount * 100.

Percent Increase = (New Amount – Original Amount) / Original Amount * 100.

Percent Decrease = (Original Amount – New Amount) / Original Amount * 100.

Amount Increase (or **Decrease**) = Original Price * Percent Markup (or Markdown).

Original Price = New Price / (Whole - Percent Markdown [or Markup]).

> **Example:** A car that was originally priced at $8300 has been reduced to $6995. What percent has it been reduced?
>
> (8300 – 6995) / 8300 * 100 = **15.72%**.

Repeated Percent Change

Increase: Final amount = Original Amount * $(1 + \text{rate})^{\text{# of changes}}$.

Decrease: Final Amount = Original Amount * $(1 - \text{rate})^{\text{# of changes}}$.

> **Example:** The weight of a tube of toothpaste decreases by 3% each time it is used. If it weighed 76.5 grams when new, what is its weight in grams after 15 uses?
>
> Final amount = $76.5 * (1 - .3)^{15}$.
>
> $76.5 * (.97)^{15} = $ **48.44 grams**.

Ratios

To solve a ratio, simply find the equivalent fraction. To distribute a whole across a ratio:

1. Total all parts.

2. Divide the whole by the total number of parts.

3. Multiply quotient by corresponding part of ratio.

> **Example:** There are 90 voters in a room, and they are either Democrat or Republican. The ratio of Democrats to Republicans is 5:4. How many Republicans are there?
>
> 1. 5 + 4 = 9.
>
> 2. 90 / 9 = 10.
>
> 3. 10 * 4 = **40 Republicans**.

Proportions

Direct Proportions: Corresponding ratio parts change in the same direction (increase/decrease).

Indirect Proportions: Corresponding ratio parts change in opposite directions (as one part increases the other decreases).

Example: A train traveling 120 miles takes 3 hours to get to its destination. How long will it take if the train travels 180 miles?

120 mph:180 mph is to x hours:3 hours. (Write as fraction and cross multiply.)
- $120/3 = 180/x$.
- $540 = 120x$.
- $x = $ **4.5 hours**.

Arithmetic Sequence

Each term is equal to the previous term plus x.

Example: 2, 5, 8, 11.
- $2 + 3 = 5; 5 + 3 = 8$ … etc.
- $x = $ **3**.

Geometric Sequence

Each term is equal to the previous term multiplied by x.

Example: 2, 4, 8, 16.
- $x = $ **2**.

Roots

Root of a Product: $\sqrt[n]{a \cdot b} = \sqrt[n]{a} \cdot \sqrt[n]{b}$.

Root of a Quotient: $\sqrt[n]{\dfrac{a}{b}} = \dfrac{\sqrt[n]{a}}{\sqrt[n]{b}}$.

Fractional Exponent: $\sqrt[n]{a^{m}} = a^{m/n}$.

Literal Equations

Equations with more than one variable. Solve in terms of one variable first.

Example: Solve for y: $4x + 3y = 3x + 2y$.

1. Combine like terms: $3y - 2y = 4x - 2x$.

2. Solve for y. $y = $ **2x**.

Linear Systems

A linear system requires the solving of two literal equations simultaneously. There are two different methods (Substitution and Addition) that can be used to solve linear systems.

Substitution Method: Solve for one variable first, and then substitute.

> **Example**: Solve for x and y: $3y - 4 + x = 0$ and $5x + 6y = 11$.

1. Solve for one variable.
   - $3y - 4 + x = 0$.
   - $3y + x = 4$.
   - $x = 4 - 3y$.

2. Substitute into second equation, and solve.
   - $5(4 - 3y) + 6y = 11$.
   - $20 - 15y + 6y = 11$.
   - $20 - 9y = 11$.
   - $-9y = -9$.
   - $y = 1$.

3. Substitute into first equation.
   - $3(1) - 4 + x = 0$.
   - $-1 + x = 0$.
   - $x = 1$.

Addition Method: Manipulate one of the equations so that when added to the other, one variable is eliminated.

> **Example**: Solve $2x + 4y = 8$ and $4x + 2y = 10$.

1. Manipulate one equation to eliminate a variable when added together.
   - $-2(2x + 4y = 8) = (-4x - 8y = -16)$.
   - $(-4x - 8y = -16) + (4x + 2y = 10)$.
   - $-6y = -6$.
   - $y = 1$.

2. Plug into an equation and solve for the other variable.
   - $2x + 4(1) = 8$.
   - $2x + 4 = 8$.
   - $2x = 4$.
   - $x = 2$.

The following is a typical word problem that would use a linear system to solve.

Example: Tommy has a collection of coins worth \$5.20. He has 8 more nickels than quarters. How many of each does he have?

1. Set up equations.
   - Let n = nickels and q = quarters.
   - $.05n + .25q = 5.2$.
   - $n = q + 8$.

2. Substitute Equation 2 into Equation 1.
   - $.05(q + 8) + .25q = 5.2$.

3. Solve for q. You can ignore the decimal point and negative sign after this step because you are solving for number of coins.
   - $-.05(q + 8) + .25q = 5.2$.
   - $.05q + .4 + .25q = 5.2$.
   - $q = 16$.

4. Plug into the original equation.
   - $n = q + 8$.
   - $n = 24$.
   - $q = 16$.

Linear Equations

An equation for a straight line. The variable CANNOT have an exponent, square roots, cube roots, etc.

Example: $y - 2x + 1$ is a straight line, with "1" being the y-intercept, and "2" being the positive slope.

Algebraic Equations

When simplifying or solving algebraic equations, you need to be able to utilize all math rules: exponents, roots, negatives, order of operations, etc.

1. Add & Subtract: Only the coefficients of like terms.

   Example: $5xy + 7y + 2yz + 11xy - 5yz = 16xy + 7y - 3yz$.

2. Multiplication: First the coefficients then the variables.

   Example: Monomial * Monomial. (Remember: a variable with no exponent has an implied exponent of 1.)
   - $(3x^4y^2z)(2y^4z^5) = 6x^4y^6z^6$.

   Example: Monomial * Polynomial.
   - $(2y^2)(y^3 + 2xy^2z + 4z) = 2y^5 + 4xy^4z + 8y^2z$

Example: Binomial * Binomial.

- $(5x + 2)(3x + 3)$. Remember: FOIL (First, Outer, Inner, Last).

  First: $5x * 3x = 15x^2$.

  Outer: $5x * 3 = 15x$.

  Inner: $2 * 3x = 6x$.

  Last: $2 * 3 = 6$.

  Combine like terms: $15x^2 + 21x + 6$.

Example: Binomial * Polynomial.

- $(x + 3)(2x^2 - 5x - 2)$.

  First Term: $x(2x^2 - 5x - 2) = 2x^3 - 5x^2 - 2x$.

  Second term: $3(2x^2 - 5x - 2) = 6x^2 - 15x - 6$.

  Added Together: $2x^3 + x^2 - 17x - 6$.

Inequalities

Inequalities are solved like linear and algebraic equations, except the sign must be reversed when dividing by a negative number.

Example: $-7x + 2 < 6 - 5x$.

Step 1 – Combine like terms: $-2x < 4$.

Step 2 – Solve for x. (Reverse the sign): $x > -2$.

Solving compound inequalities will give you two answers.

Example: $-4 \leq 2x - 2 \leq 6$.

Step 1 – Add 2 to each term to isolate x: $-2 \leq 2x \leq 8$.

Step 2: Divide by 2: $-1 \leq x \leq 4$.

Solution set is **[-1, 4]**.

Exponent Rules

Rule	Example
$x^0 = 1$	$5^0 = 1$
$x^1 = x$	$5^1 = 5$
$x^a \cdot x^b = x^{a+b}$	$5^2 * 5^3 = 5^5$
$(xy)^a = x^a y^a$	$(5 * 6)^2 = 5^2 * 6^2 = 25 * 36$
$(x^a)^b = x^{ab}$	$(5^2)^3 = 5^6$
$(x/y)^a = x^a/y^a$	$(10/5)^2 = 10^2/5^2 = 100/25$
$x^a/y^b = x^{a-b}$	$5^4/5^3 = 5^1 = 5$ (remember $x \neq 0$)
$x^{1/a} = \sqrt[a]{x}$	$25^{1/2} = \sqrt[2]{25} = 5$
$x^{-a} = \dfrac{1}{x^a}$	$5^{-2} = \dfrac{1}{5^2} = \dfrac{1}{25}$ (remember $x \neq 0$)
$(-x)^a$ = positive number if "a" is even; negative number if "a" is odd.	

Slope

The formula used to calculate the slope (m) of a straight line connecting two points is: $m = (y_2 - y_1) / (x_2 - x_1)$ = change in y / change in x.

Example: Calculate slope of the line in the diagram.

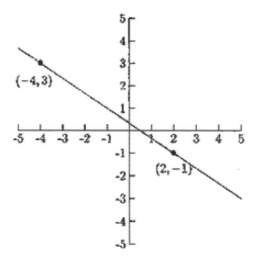

$m = (3 - (-1))/(-4 - 2) = 4/-6 = $ **- 2/3**.

Midpoint

To determine the midpoint between two points, simply add the two x coordinates together and divide by 2 (midpoint x). Then add the y coordinates together and divide by 2 (midpoint y).

$$\left(\frac{x_1 + x_2}{2}, \frac{y_1 + y}{2} \right)$$

23

Fundamental Counting Principle

(The number of possibilities of an event happening) * (the number of possibilities of another event happening) = the total number of possibilities.

Example: If you take a multiple choice test with 5 questions, with 4 answer choices for each question, how many test result possibilities are there?

Solution: Question 1 has 4 choices; question 2 has 4 choices; etc.

4 *4 * 4 * 4 * 4 (one for each question) = **1024 possible test results**.

Permutations

The number of ways a set number of items can be arranged. Recognized by the use of a factorial ($n!$), with n being the number of items.

If $n = 3$, then $3! = 3 * 2 * 1 = 6$. If you need to arrange n number of things but x number are alike, then $n!$ is divided by $x!$

Example: How many different ways can the letters in the word **balance** be arranged?

Solution: There are 7 letters, so $n! = 7!$ But 2 letters are the same, so $x! = 2!$ Set up the equation:
$$\frac{7 * 6 * 5 * 4 * 3 * 2 * 1}{2 * 1} = 2540 \textbf{ ways}.$$

Combinations

To calculate total number of possible combinations, use the formula: $n!/r! \, (n-r)!$
Where n = # of objects; and r = # of objects selected at a time.

Example: If seven people are selected in groups of three, how many different combinations are possible?

Solution:
$$\frac{7 * 6 * 5 * 4 * 3 * 2 * 1}{(3 * 2 * 1)(7 - 3)} = 210 \textbf{ possible combinations}.$$

Functions and Their Rules

Functions are simple if you think of them as just another substitution problem. Pay attention to your math, always double check your signs, and check your answer.

Function	Rule	Example
Adding	$(f + g)(x) = f(x) + g(x)$.	If $f(x) = 3x + 2$ and $g(x) = x^2$, then $(f + g)(x) = 3x + 2 + x^2$.
Subtracting	$(f - g)(x) = f(x) - g(x)$.	If $f(x) = 3x + 2$ and $g(x) = x^2$, then $(f - g)(x) = 3x + 2 - x^2$.
Multiplying	$(f * g)(x) = f(x) * g(x)$.	If $f(x) = 3x + 2$ and $g(x) = x^2$, then $(f * g)(x) = (3x + 2) * x^2$.
Dividing	$(f / g)(x) = f(x) / g(x)$, provided $g(x) \neq 0$.	If $f(x) = 3x + 2$ and $g(x) = x^2$, then $(f / g)(x) = (3x + 2) / x^2$.
Composition	$(f \circ g)(x) = f(g(x))$. [Replace each x in the formula of $f(x)$ with the entire formula of $g(x)$.]	If $f(x) = x^2 - x$ and $g(x) = x - 4$, then: $(f \circ g)(x) = f(g(x))$ $= f(x - 4)$ $= (x - 4)^2 - (x - 4)$. (Can be reduced further.)　　$(g \circ f)(x) = g(f(x))$ $= g(x^2 - x)$ $= (x^2 - x) - 4$. (Can be reduced further.)
Inverse	$f^{-1}(x) =$ the inverse of (x); denoted by $f(f^{-1}(x)) = f^{-1}(f(x)) = x$.	If two functions, $f(x)$ and $g(x)$, are defined so that $(f \circ g)(x) = x$ and $(g \circ f)(x) = x$, then $f(x)$ and $g(x)$ are inverse functions of each other.

Strategies for Inverse Functions

To find the correct inverse function of $f(x)$ every time, you can use this procedure:

Given the function $f(x)$, we want to find the inverse function, $f\text{-}1(x)$.

1. First, replace $f(x)$ with y. This is done to make the rest of the process easier.

2. Replace every x with a y and replace every y with an x.

3. Solve the equation from Step 2 for y. This is the step where mistakes are most often made so be careful with this step.

4. Replace y with $f\text{-}1(x)$. In other words, we've managed to find the inverse at this point.

Example: If $f(x) = \frac{x-1}{x+1}$, find $f^{-1}(x)$.

1. $y = \frac{x-1}{x+1}$

2. $x = \frac{y-1}{y+1}$

3. $xy + x = y - 1$
$xy - y = -x - 1$
$y(x - 1) = -(x + 1)$
$y = \frac{-(x+1)}{(x-1)}$

4. $f^{-1}(x) = \frac{-(x+1)}{(x-1)}$

The following is an example of a typical function problem, followed by function rules and definitions you need to know.

If $f(x) = x^2 + 3x$, find $f(x + 2)$.

1. Simply replace $(x + 2)$ for x in the first equation $(x^2 + 3x)$.
   - $(x + 2)^2 + 3(x + 2)$.

2. Use FOIL for first term.
   - $x^2 + 4x + 4 + 3x + 6$.

3. Combine like terms: $x^2 + 7x + 10$.

4. Factor: $(x + 5)(x + 2)$.

5. Set equations to zero. Solve.
   - $x + 5 = 0; x = -5$.
   - $x + 2 = 0; x = -2$.

Quadratics

Factoring: converting $ax^2 + bx + c$ to factored form. Find two numbers that are factors of c and whose sum is b.

Example: Factor $2x^2 + 12x + 18 = 0$.

1. If possible, factor out a common monomial: $2(x^2 - 6x + 9)$.

2. Find two numbers that are factors of 9; and also sum to -6: $2(x - \_)(x - \_)$.

3. Fill in the binomials. Be sure to check your answer and signs: $2(x - 3)(x - 3)$.

4. To solve, set each to $= 0$: $x - 3 = 0; x = 3$.

If the equation cannot be factored (there are no two factors of c that sum to $= b$), the quadratic formula is used.

$$x = \frac{-b \pm \sqrt{b^2 - 4ac}}{2a}$$

Using the same equation from the above example: $a = 2$, $b = 12$, and $c = 18$. Plug into the formula and solve. Remember there will still be two answers due to the (+) and (-) before the radical.

Graphing

You must be familiar with all the various aspects of graphing functions and quadratics, especially the following concepts:

Vertex: The turning point; can be the minimum or the maximum.
Has the coordinates (h, k). The vertex form of the quadratic equation is:

$$f(x) = a(x - h)^2 + k. \quad \text{[The vertex is at } (h, k).]$$

The formula $(\frac{-b}{2a}, f(\frac{-b}{2a}))$ (correspond with the quadratic equation) can be used to find the vertex.

Axis of Symmetry: The line that runs through the vertex. The formula used is the same as finding for h above: $h = \frac{-b}{2a}$.

Roots, Zeros, and Solutions: All the values of x which make the equation equal to zero, also known as x-intercepts.

Domain: All the possible x values of a function.

Range: All the possible output values ($f(x)$ or y values) of the function.
Translations: Translations follow these rules:

- $f(x) + k$ is $f(x)$ shifted upward k units.
- $f(x) - k$ is $f(x)$ shifted downward k units.
- $f(x + h)$ is $f(x)$ shifted left h units.
- $f(x - h)$ is $f(x)$ shifted right h units.
- $-f(x)$ is $f(x)$ flipped upside down ("reflected about the x-axis").
- $f(-x)$ is the mirror of $f(x)$ ("reflected about the y-axis").
- The graph of $y = f(x - h) + k$ is the translation of the graph – d $y = f(x)$ – by (h, k) units in the plane.

Geometry

- **Acute Angle**: Measures less than 90°.

- **Acute Triangle**: Each angle measures less than 90°.

- **Obtuse Angle**: Measures greater than 90°.

- **Obtuse Triangle**: One angle measures greater than 90°.

- **Adjacent Angles**: Share a side and a vertex.

- **Complementary Angles**: Adjacent angles that sum to 90°.

- **Supplementary Angles**: Adjacent angles that sum to 180°.

- **Vertical Angles**: Angles that are opposite of each other. They are always congruent (equal in measure).

- **Equilateral Triangle**: All angles are equal.

- **Isosceles Triangle**: Two sides and two angles are equal.

- **Scalene**: No equal angles.

- **Parallel Lines**: Lines that will never intersect. Y **ll** X means line Y is parallel to line X.

- **Perpendicular lines**: Lines that intersect or cross to form 90° angles.

- **Transversal Line**: A line that crosses parallel lines.

- **Bisector**: Any line that cuts a line segment, angle, or polygon exactly in half.

- **Polygon**: Any enclosed plane shape with three or more connecting sides (ex. a triangle).

- **Regular Polygon**: Has all equal sides and equal angles (ex. square).

- **Arc**: A portion of a circle's edge.

- **Chord**: A line segment that connects two different points on a circle.

- **Tangent**: Something that touches a circle at only one point without crossing through it.

- **Sum of Angles**: The sum of angles of a polygon can be calculated using $(n-1)180^\circ$, when n = the number of sides.

Know the Names of Sided Plane Figures:

Number of Sides	Name	Number of Sides	Name
3	Triangle (or Trigon)	11	Hendecagon
4	Quadrilateral (or Tetragon)	12	Dodecagon
5	Pentagon	13	Tridecagon
6	Hexagon	14	Tetradecagon
7	Heptagon	15	Pentadecagon
8	Octagon	16	Hexadecagon
9	Nonagon	17	Heptadecagon

Triangles

The angles in a triangle add up to 180°.
Area of a triangle = ½ * b * h, or ½bh.
Pythagoras' Theorem: $a^2 + b^2 = c^2$.

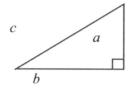

Regular Polygons

Polygon Angle Principle: $S = (n - 2)180$, where S = the sum of interior angles of a polygon with n-sides.

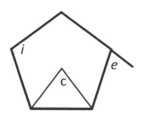

The measure of each central angle (c) is $360°/n$.
The measure of each interior angle (i) is $(n - 2)180°/n$.
The measure of each exterior angle (e) is $360°/n$.
To compare areas of similar polygons: $A_1/A_2 = (side_1/side_2)^2$

Trapezoids

Four-sided polygon, in which the bases (and only the bases) are parallel.

Isosceles Trapezoid: Base angles are congruent.

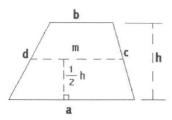

Area and Perimeter of a Trapezoid

$$m = \frac{1}{2}(a+b)$$

$$Area = \frac{1}{2}h*(a+b) = m*h$$

$$Perimeter = a+b+c+d = 2m+c+d$$

If m is the median then: $m \parallel \overline{AB}$ and $m \parallel \overline{CD}$

Rhombus

Four-sided polygon, in which all four sides are congruent and opposite sides are parallel.

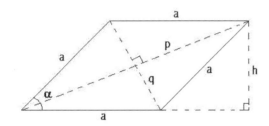

Area and Perimeter of a Rhombus

$$Perimeter = 4a$$

$$Area = a^2 \sin\alpha = a*h = \frac{1}{2}pq$$

$$4a^2 = p^2 + q^2$$

Rectangle

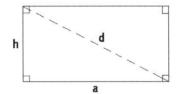

Area and Perimeter of a Rectangle

$$d = \sqrt{a^2 + h^2}$$

$$a = \sqrt{d^2 - h^2}$$

$$h = \sqrt{d^2 - a^2}$$

$$Perimeter = 2a + 2h$$

$$Area = a \cdot h$$

Square

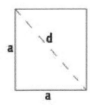

Area and Perimeter of a Square

$$d = a\sqrt{2}$$

$$Perimeter = 4a = 2d\sqrt{2}$$

$$Area = a^2 = \frac{1}{2}d^2$$

Circle

Area and Perimeter of a Circle

$$d = 2r$$

$$Perimeter = 2\pi r = \pi d$$

$$Area = \pi r^2$$

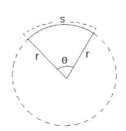

The product length of one chord equals the product length of the other, or:

AB=CD

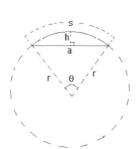

Area and Perimeter of the Sector of a Circle

$$\alpha = \frac{\theta\pi}{180} \ (rad)$$

$$s = r\alpha$$

$$Perimeter = 2r + s$$

$$Area = \frac{1}{2}\theta \, r^2 \ (radians) \ or \ \frac{n}{360}\pi r^2$$

$$length \ (l) \ of \ an \ arc \ \ l = \frac{\pi n r}{180} \ or \ \frac{n}{360} \, 2\pi r$$

Area and Perimeter of the Segment of a Circle

$$\alpha = \frac{\theta\pi}{180} \ (rad)$$

$$a = 2\sqrt{2hr - h^2}$$

$$a^2 = 2r^2 - 2r^2\cos\theta$$

$$s = r\alpha$$

$$h = r - \frac{1}{2}\sqrt{4r^2 - a^2}$$

$$Perimeter = a + s$$

$$Area = \frac{1}{2}[sr - a(r - h)]$$

Cube

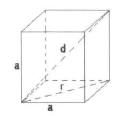

Area and Volume of a Cube

$$r = a\sqrt{2}$$

$$d = a\sqrt{3}$$

$$Area = 6a^2$$

$$Volume = a^3$$

Cuboid

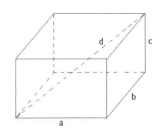

Area and Volume of a Cuboid

$$d = \sqrt{a^2 + b^2 + c^2}$$

$$A = 2(ab + ac + bc)$$

$$V = abc$$

Pyramid

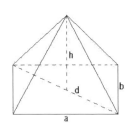

Area and Volume of a Pyramid

$$A_{lateral} = a\sqrt{h^2 + \left(\frac{b}{2}\right)^2} + b\sqrt{h^2 + \left(\frac{a}{2}\right)^2}$$

$$d = \sqrt{a^2 + b^2}$$

$$A_{base} = ab$$

$$A_{total} = A_{lateral} + A_{base}$$

$$V = \frac{1}{3}abh$$

Cylinder

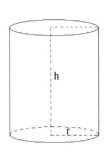

Area and Volume of a Cylinder

$$d = 2r$$

$$A_{surface} = 2\pi rh$$

$$A_{base} = 2\pi r^2$$

$$Area = A_{surface} + A_{base}$$

$$= 2\pi r\,(h + r)$$

$$Volume = \pi r^2 h$$

Cone

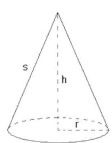

Area and Volume of a Cone

$$d = 2r$$

$$A_{surface} = \pi rs$$

$$A_{base} = \pi r^2$$

$$Area = A_{surface} + A_{base}$$

$$= 2\pi r\,(h + r)$$

$$Volume = \frac{1}{3}\pi r^2 h$$

Chapter 2: Reading Comprehension

In the Reading section of the exam, you will be presented with various texts, ranging from 300 to 800 words in length, each with related questions for you to answer. The test measures your ability to comprehend and reason about the passage's subject and message. There are three types of basic questions you will encounter:

1. **Vocabulary in Context**: You will be asked to provide the author's intended meaning of a word. (Watch out! In many cases, words will have different meanings from their "dictionary" definitions. Make sure you take the word's context into account.)

2. **Literal Comprehension**: You will be asked questions regarding what the passage directly states.

3. **Extended Reasoning**: Most of the questions will be this type. They'll ask questions such as: "What is the author's tone? What is being inferred? What is the main idea?"

Strategies for the Reading Section

1. If you have the opportunity, first read any passages that cover subjects which are interesting or familiar to you (even if they are the last passages). You are more likely to do well when reading about something you find interesting.

2. Pay attention to how paragraphs begin and end. CASA passages are written in general English prose – the topic sentence usually at the very beginning, and the main point usually at the end. You can then skim the material in-between.

3. You may need to return to the passage to find your answers. Therefore, as you're reading, make short notes beside certain passages to make important information easier to find.

4. Unless the answer comes immediately to mind, save the questions that require you to return to the passage for last. Answering the general questions first will maximize your points.

5. Don't use any previous knowledge you may have to answer the questions – only use the information presented in the passage.

6. Although you can decide the order in which to read the passages, don't jump between the questions. Answer each passage's questions separately. If you leave a passage before completing all the questions that you can, you will have to reread the passage later when you come back to it, which is a time-killer.

7. An answer choice can be factually true but not necessarily correct. The actual answer will be the one which best answers the question according to the passage.

8. Educated guesses narrow down your answer choices – use them if you are unsure about a question.

9. Practice! The only way to improve is to practice critical reading.

With that said, let's begin the review!

The Main Idea

Finding and understanding the main idea of a text is an essential reading skill. When you look past the facts and information and get to the heart of what the writer is trying to say, that's the **main idea**.

Imagine that you're at a friend's home for the evening:

> "Here," he says, "Let's watch this movie."

> "Sure," you reply. "What's it about?"

You'd like to know a little about what you'll be watching, but your question may not get you a satisfactory answer, because you've only asked about the subject of the film. The subject—what the movie is about—is only half the story. Think, for example, about all the alien invasion films ever been made. While these films may share the same general subject, what they have to say about the aliens or about humanity's theoretical response to invasion may be very different. Each film has different ideas it wants to convey about a subject, just as writers write because they have something they want to say about a particular subject. When you look beyond the facts and information to what the writer really wants to say about his or her subject, you're looking for the main idea.

One of the most common questions on reading comprehension exams is, "What is the main idea of this passage?" How would you answer this question for the paragraph below?

> "Wilma Rudolph, the crippled child who became an Olympic running champion, is an inspiration for us all. Born prematurely in 1940, Wilma spent her childhood battling illness, including measles, scarlet fever, chicken pox, pneumonia, and polio, a crippling disease which at that time had no cure. At the age of four, she was told she would never walk again. But Wilma and her family refused to give up. After years of special treatment and physical therapy, 12-year-old Wilma was able to walk normally again. But walking wasn't enough for Wilma, who was determined to be an athlete. Before long, her talent earned her a spot in the 1956 Olympics, where she earned a bronze medal. In the 1960 Olympics, the height of her career, she won three gold medals."

What is the main idea of this paragraph? You might be tempted to answer, "Wilma Rudolph" or "Wilma Rudolph's life." Yes, Wilma Rudolph's life is the **subject** of the passage—who or what the passage is about—but the subject is not necessarily the main idea. The **main idea** is what the writer wants to say about this subject. What is the main thing the writer says about Wilma's life?

Which of the following statements is the main idea of the paragraph?

> a) Wilma Rudolph was very sick as a child.
> b) Wilma Rudolph was an Olympic champion.
> c) Wilma Rudolph is someone to admire.

Main idea: The overall fact, feeling, or thought a writer wants to convey about his or her subject.

The best answer is **c)**: Wilma Rudolph is someone to admire. This is the idea the paragraph adds up to; it's what holds all of the information in the paragraph together.

This example also shows two important characteristics of a main idea:

1. It is **general** enough to encompass all of the ideas in the passage.

2. It is an **assertion.** An assertion is a statement made by the writer.

The main idea of a passage must be general enough to encompass all of the ideas in the passage. It should be broad enough for all of the other sentences in that passage to fit underneath it, like people under an umbrella. Notice that the first two options, "Wilma Rudolph was very sick as a child" and "Wilma Rudolph was an Olympic champion", are too specific to be the main idea. They aren't broad enough to cover all of the ideas in the passage, because the passage talks about both her illnesses and her Olympic achievements. Only the third answer is general enough to be the main idea of the paragraph.

A main idea is also some kind of **assertion** about the subject. An assertion is a claim that something is true. Assertions can be facts or opinions, but in either case, an assertion should be supported by specific ideas, facts, and details. In other words, the main idea makes a general assertion that tells readers that something is true.

The supporting sentences, on the other hand, show readers that this assertion is true by providing specific facts and details. For example, in the Wilma Rudolph paragraph, the writer makes a general assertion: "Wilma Rudolph, the crippled child who became an Olympic running champion, is an inspiration for us all." The other sentences offer specific facts and details that prove why Wilma Rudolph is an inspirational person.

Writers often state their main ideas in one or two sentences so that readers can have a very clear understanding about the main point of the passage. A sentence that expresses the main idea of a paragraph is called a **topic sentence.**
Notice, for example, how the first sentence in the Wilma Rudolph paragraph states the main idea:

> "Wilma Rudolph, the crippled child who became an Olympic running champion, is an inspiration for us all."

This sentence is therefore the topic sentence for the paragraph. Topic sentences are often found at the beginning of paragraphs. Sometimes, though, writers begin with specific supporting ideas and lead up to the main idea, and in this case the topic sentence is often found at the end of the paragraph. Sometimes the topic sentence is even found somewhere in the middle, and other times there isn't a clear topic sentence at all—but that doesn't mean there isn't a main idea; the author has just chosen not to express it in a clear topic sentence. In this last case, you'll have to look carefully at the paragraph for clues about the main idea.

Main Ideas vs. Supporting Ideas

If you're not sure whether something is a main idea or a supporting idea, ask yourself the following question: is the sentence making a **general statement,** or is it providing **specific information?** In the Wilma Rudolph paragraph above, for example, all of the sentences except the first make specific statements. They are not general enough to serve as an umbrella or net for the whole paragraph.

Writers often provide clues that can help you distinguish between main ideas and their supporting ideas. Here are some of the most common words and phrases used to introduce specific examples:

1. **For example…**

2. **Specifically…**

3. **In addition…**

4. **Furthermore…**

5. **For instance…**

6. **Others…**

7. **In particular…**

8. **Some…**

These signal words tell you that a supporting fact or idea will follow. If you're having trouble finding the main idea of a paragraph, try eliminating sentences that begin with these phrases, because they will most likely be too specific to be a main ideas.

Implied Main Idea

When the main idea is **implied**, there's no topic sentence, which means that finding the main idea requires some detective work. But don't worry! You already know the importance of structure, word choice, style, and tone. Plus, you know how to read carefully to find clues, and you know that these clues will help you figure out the main idea.

For Example:

"One of my summer reading books was *The Windows of Time*. Though it's more than 100 pages long, I read it in one afternoon. I couldn't wait to see what happened to Evelyn, the main character. But by the time I got to the end, I wondered if I should have spent my afternoon doing something else. The ending was so awful that I completely forgot that I'd enjoyed most of the book."

There's no topic sentence here, but you should still be able to find the main idea. Look carefully at what the writer says and how she says it. What is she suggesting?

a) *The Windows of Time* is a terrific novel.
b) *The Windows of Time* is disappointing.
c) *The Windows of Time* is full of suspense.
d) *The Windows of Time* is a lousy novel.

The correct answer is **b)** – the novel is disappointing. How can you tell that this is the main idea? First, we can eliminate choice **c)**, because it's too specific to be a main idea. It deals only with one specific aspect of the novel (its suspense).

Sentences **a)**, **b)**, and **d)**, on the other hand, all express a larger idea – a general assertion about the quality of the novel. But only one of these statements can actually serve as a "net" for the whole paragraph. Notice that while the first few sentences praise the novel, the last two criticize it. Clearly, this is a mixed review.

Therefore, the best answer is **b)**. Sentence **a)** is too positive and doesn't account for the "awful" ending. Sentence **d)**, on the other hand, is too negative and doesn't account for the reader's sense of suspense and interest in the main character. But sentence **b)** allows for both positive and negative aspects – when a good thing turns bad, we often feel disappointed.

Now let's look at another example. Here, the word choice will be more important, so read carefully.

> "Fortunately, none of Toby's friends had ever seen the apartment where Toby lived with his mother and sister. Sandwiched between two burnt-out buildings, his two-story apartment building was by far the ugliest one on the block. It was a real eyesore: peeling orange paint (orange!), broken windows, crooked steps, crooked everything. He could just imagine what his friends would say if they ever saw this poor excuse for a building."

Which of the following expresses the main idea of this paragraph?

    a) Toby wishes he could move to a nicer building.
    b) Toby wishes his dad still lived with them.
    c) Toby is glad none of his friends know where he lives.
    d) Toby is sad because he doesn't have any friends.

From the description, we can safely assume that Toby doesn't like his apartment building and wishes he could move to a nicer building **a)**. But that idea isn't general enough to cover the whole paragraph, because it's about his building.

Because the first sentence states that Toby has friends, the answer cannot be **d)**. We know that Toby lives only with his mother and little sister, so we might assume that he wishes his dad still lived with them, **b)**, but there's nothing in the paragraph to support that assumption, and this idea doesn't include the two main topics of the paragraph—Toby's building and Toby's friends.

What the paragraph adds up to is that Toby is terribly embarrassed about his building, and he's glad that none of his friends have seen it **c)**. This is the main idea. The paragraph opens with the word "fortunately," so we know that he thinks it's a good thing none of his friends have been to his house. Plus, notice how the building is described: "by far the ugliest on the block," which says a lot since it's stuck "between two burnt-out buildings." The writer calls it an "eyesore," and repeats "orange" with an exclamation point to emphasize how ugly the color is. Everything is "crooked" in this "poor excuse for a building." Toby is clearly ashamed of where he lives and worries about what his friends would think if they saw it.

Cause and Effect

Understanding cause and effect is important for reading success. Every event has at least one cause (what made it happen) and at least one effect (the result of what happened). Some events have more than one cause, and some have more than one effect. An event is also often part of a chain of causes and effects. Causes and effects are usually signaled by important transitional words and phrases.

Words Indicating Cause:

1. **Because (of)**

2. **Created (by)**

3. **Caused (by)**

4. **Since**

Words Indicating Effect:

1. **As a result**

2. **Since**

3. **Consequently**

4. **So**

5. **Hence**

6. **Therefore**

Sometimes, a writer will offer his or her opinion about why an event happened when the facts of the cause(s) aren't clear. Or a writer may predict what he or she thinks will happen because of a certain event (its effects). If this is the case, you need to consider how reasonable those opinions are. Are the writer's ideas logical? Does the writer offer support for the conclusions he or she offers?

Reading Between the Lines

Paying attention to word choice is particularly important when the main idea of a passage isn't clear. A writer's word choice doesn't just affect meaning; it also creates it. For example, look at the following description from a teacher's evaluation of a student applying to a special foreign language summer camp. There's no topic sentence, but if you use your powers of observation, you should be able to tell how the writer feels about her subject.

> "As a student, Jane usually completes her work on time and checks it carefully. She speaks French well and is learning to speak with less of an American accent. She has often been a big help to other students who are just beginning to learn the language."

What message does this passage send about Jane? Is she the best French student the writer has ever had? Is she one of the worst, or is she just average? To answer these questions, you have to make an inference, and you must support your inference with specific observations. What makes you come to the conclusion that you come to?

The **diction** of the paragraph above reveals that this is a positive evaluation, but not a glowing recommendation.

40

Here are some of the specific observations you might have made to support this conclusion:

- The writer uses the word "usually" in the first sentence. This means that Jane is good about meeting deadlines for work, but not great; she doesn't always hand in her work on time.

- The first sentence also says that Jane checks her work carefully. While Jane may sometimes hand in work late, at least she always makes sure it's quality work. She's not sloppy.

- The second sentence tells us she's "learning to speak with less of an American accent." This suggests that she has a strong accent and needs to improve in this area. It also suggests, though, that she is already making progress.

- The third sentence tells us that she "often" helps "students who are just beginning to learn the language." From this we can conclude that Jane has indeed mastered the basics. Otherwise, how could she be a big help to students who are just starting to learn? By looking at the passage carefully, then, you can see how the writer feels about her subject.

Chapter 3: The Writing Section

MULTIPLE-CHOICE

The multiple-choice questions in the Writing section will cover: Error Identification, in which you'll need to recognize errors in sentence structure, grammar, and syntax; Sentence Improvement, wherein, as the name suggests, you will be given choices to improve a presented sentence; and Paragraph Improvement, which will test your ability to revise sentences in a larger context.

Many of the concepts which you reviewed in the previous chapter are applicable to this chapter as well. We'll provide a brief review of those concepts with which you'll need to be familiar that were not covered in Chapter 2.

Nouns, Pronouns, Verbs, Adjectives, and Adverbs

Nouns
Nouns are people, places, or things. They are typically the subject of a sentence. For example, "The hospital was very clean." The noun is "hospital;" it is the "place."

Pronouns
Pronouns essentially "replace" nouns. This allows a sentence to not sound repetitive. Take the sentence: "Sam stayed home from school because Sam was not feeling well." The word "Sam" appears twice in the same sentence. Instead, you can use a pronoun and say, "Sam stayed at home because *he* did not feel well." Sounds much better, right?

Most Common Pronouns:

- I, me, mine, my.

- You, your, yours.

- He, him, his.

- She, her, hers.

- It, its.

- We, us, our, ours.

- They, them, their, theirs.

Verbs
Remember the old commercial, "Verb: It's what you do"? That sums up verbs in a nutshell! Verbs are the "action" of a sentence; verbs "do" things.

They can, however, be quite tricky. Depending on the subject of a sentence, the tense of the word (past, present, future, etc.), and whether or not they are regular or irregular, verbs have many variations.

Example: "He runs to second base." The verb is "runs." This is a "regular verb."

Example: "I am 7 years old." The verb in this case is "am." This is an "irregular verb."

As mentioned, verbs must use the correct tense – and that tense must remain the same throughout the sentence. "I was baking cookies and eat some dough." That sounded strange, didn't it? That's because the two verbs "baking" and "eat" are presented in different tenses. "Was baking" occurred in the past; "eat," on the other hand, occurs in the present. Instead, it should be "**ate** some dough."

Adjectives

Adjectives are words that describe a noun and give more information. Take the sentence: "The boy hit the ball." If you want to know more about the noun "boy," then you could use an adjective to describe it. "The **little** boy hit the ball." An adjective simply provides more information about a noun or subject in a sentence.

Adverb

For some reason, many people have a difficult time with adverbs – but don't worry! They are really quite simple. Adverbs are similar to adjectives in that they provide more information about a part of a sentence; however, they do **not** describe nouns – that's an adjective's job. Instead, adverbs describe verbs, adjectives, and even other adverbs.

Take the sentence: "The doctor said she hired a new employee."

It would give more information to say: "The doctor said she **recently** hired a new employee." Now we know more about *how* the action was executed. Adverbs typically describe when or how something has happened, how it looks, how it feels, etc.

Good vs. Well

A very common mistake that people make concerning adverbs is the misuse of the word "good."

"Good" is an adjective – things taste good, look good, and smell good. "Good" can even be a noun – "Superman does good" – when the word is speaking about "good" vs. "evil." HOWEVER, "good" is never an adverb.

People commonly say things like, "I did really good on that test," or, "I'm good." Ugh! This is NOT the correct way to speak! In those sentences, the word "good" is being used to describe an action: how a person **did**, or how a person **is**. Therefore, the adverb "well" should be used. "I did really **well** on that test." "I'm **well**."

The correct use of "well" and "good" can make or break a person's impression of your grammar – make sure to always speak correctly!

Study Tips for Improving Vocabulary and Grammar

1. You're probably pretty computer savvy and know the Internet very well. Visit the Online Writing Lab website, which is sponsored by Purdue University, at http://owl.english.purdue.edu. This site provides you with an excellent overview of syntax, writing style, and strategy. It also has helpful and lengthy review sections that include multiple-choice "Test Your Knowledge" quizzes, which provide immediate answers to the questions.

2. It's beneficial to read the entire passage first to determine its intended meaning BEFORE you attempt to answer any questions. Doing so provides you with key insight into a passage's syntax (especially verb tense, subject-verb agreement, modifier placement, writing style, and punctuation).

3. When you answer a question, use the "Process-of-Elimination Method" to determine the best answer. Try each of the four answers and determine which one BEST fits with the meaning of the paragraph. Find the BEST answer. Chances are that the BEST answer is the CORRECT answer.

Practice Sentence Improvement

To give you a better idea of what you can expect from this section of the CASA, here are a few sample sentence improvement questions.

Paragraph A
(1) Of the two types of eclipses, the most common is the lunar eclipse, which occurs when a full moon passes through Earth's shadow. (2) The disc-shaped moon slowly disappears completely or turns a coppery red color. (3) Solar and lunar eclipses both occur from time to time.

Paragraph B
(4) During a solar eclipse, the moon passes between the Earth and Sun. (5) As the moon moves into alignment, it blocks the light from the Sun creating an eerie darkness. (6) When the moon is perfectly in position, the Sun's light is visible as a ring, or corona, around the dark disc of the moon. (7) A lunar eclipse can be viewed from anywhere on the nighttime half of Earth, a solar eclipse can only be viewed from a zone that is only about 200 miles wide and covers about one-half of a percent of Earth's total area.

1. Sentence 1: "Of the two types of eclipses, the most common is the lunar eclipse, which occurs when a full moon passes through Earth's shadow." What correction should be made to this sentence?
    a) Change "most" to "more."
    b) Change "occurs" to "occur."
    c) Change "which" to "that."
    d) Change "Earth's" to "Earths'."
    e) No correction is necessary.

2. Sentence 2: "The disc-shaped moon slowly disappears completely or turns a coppery red color." If you rewrote sentence 2, beginning with "<u>The disc-shaped moon slowly turns a coppery red color</u>," the next word should be:
   a) And.
   b) But.
   c) When.
   d) Because.
   e) Or.

3. Which revision would improve the effectiveness of paragraph A?
   a) Remove sentence 1.
   b) Move sentence 2 to the beginning of the paragraph.
   c) Remove sentence 2.
   d) Move sentence 3 to the beginning of the paragraph.
   e) No revision is necessary.

4. Sentence 7: "A lunar eclipse can be viewed from anywhere on the nighttime half of <u>Earth, a solar eclipse</u> can only be viewed from a zone that is only about 200 miles wide and covers about one-half of a percent of Earth's total area." Which of the following is the best way to write the underlined portion of this sentence? If the original is the best way, choose option **a)**.
   a) "Earth, a solar eclipse"
   b) "Earth a solar eclipse"
   c) "Earth; a solar eclipse"
   d) "Earth, because a solar eclipse"
   e) "Earth, when a solar eclipse"

Answers:

1. **a)**
   Use the comparative "more" when comparing only two things. Here, you comparing two types of eclipses, so "more" is correct. The other changes introduce errors.

2. **e)**
   The clauses are joined by the conjunction "or" in the original sentence. Maintaining this conjunction maintains the original relationship between ideas.

3. **d)**
   As sentence 3 would serve as a good topic sentence, as well as an effective lead into sentence 1, the paragraph could be improved by moving sentence 3 to the beginning.

4. **c)**
   The two related sentences should be separated by a semicolon. The other answers introduce incorrect punctuation or an inaccurate relationship between the sentences.

THE WRITING SAMPLE

During this portion of the test, you will be provided a prompt, for which you will need to write a short response essay. You will need to write an essay that is focused, organized, well-developed and supported, free of errors (usage, spelling, mechanics), and that has proper sentence structure.

This may sound like a tall order, but you can do it! The only way to prepare for this section is to practice writing timed essays. Your essay will be read by two different people, and given two separate scores from 1 to 6 (6 being the highest). If the response is so unrelated to the topic, is illegible, or even written in a language other than English, the section will not receive a grade.

An Effective Essay Demonstrates:

1. Insightful and effective development of a point-of-view on the issue.

2. Critical thinking skills. For example: Two oppositions are given; instead of siding with one, you provide examples in which both would be appropriate.

3. Organization. It is clearly focused and displays a smooth progression of ideas.

4. Supportive information. If a statement is made, it is followed by examples, reasons, or other supporting evidence.

5. Skillful use of varied, accurate, and apt vocabulary.

6. Sentence variety. (Not every sentence follows a "subject-verb" pattern. Mix it up!)

7. Proper grammar and spelling.

Essay Examples and Evaluations

Here we will provide a sample essay prompt, followed by four short sample responses. The four sample responses each display different qualities of work; an explanation will follow each sample, explaining what score it would have earned and why.

Prompt:
Research tells us that what children learn in their earliest years is very important to their future success in school. Because of this, public schools all over the country are starting to offer Pre-Kindergarten classes.

What are the benefits of starting school early? What are some of the problems you see in sending four-year-olds to school?

Write a composition in which you weigh the pros and cons of public school education for Pre-Kindergartners. Give reasons and specific examples to support your opinion. There is no specific word limit for your composition, but it should be long enough to give a clear and complete presentation of your ideas.

Sample Score 5-6 Essay

Today, more and more four-year-olds are joining their big brothers and sisters on the school bus and going to Pre-Kindergarten. Although the benefits of starting school early are clear, it is also clear that Pre-K is not for every child.

The students who are successful in Pre-K are ahead when they start kindergarten. Pre-K teaches them to play well with others. Even though it does not teach skills like reading and writing, it does help to prepare students for "real" school. Pre-K students sing songs, dance, paint and draw, climb and run. They learn to share and to follow directions. They tell stories and answer questions, and as they do, they add new words to their vocabularies. Pre-K can also give students experiences they might not get at home. They might take trips to the zoo or the farm, have visits from musicians or scientists, and so on. These experiences help the students better understand the world.

There are, however, some real differences among children of this age. Some four-year-olds are just not ready for the structure of school life. Some have a hard time leaving home, even for only three or four hours a day. Other children may already be getting a great preschool education at home or in daycare.

While you weigh the advantages and disadvantages of Pre-K, it is safe to say that each child is different. For some children, it is a wonderful introduction to the world of school. But others may not or should not be forced to attend Pre-K.

Evaluation of Sample Score 5-6 Essay
This paper is clearly organized and has stated a definite point of view. The paper opens with an introduction and closes with a conclusion. The introduction and conclusion combine an expression of the writer's opinion. Connections to the writer's opinion are made throughout the paper.

Sample Score 3-4 Essay

Just like everything in life, there are pros and cons to early childhood education. Pre-K classes work for many children, but they aren't for everyone. The plusses of Pre-K are obvious. Pre-K children learn many skills that will help them in kindergarten and later on. Probably the most important thing they learn is how to follow directions. This is a skill they will need at all stages of their life.

Other plusses include simple tasks like cutting, coloring in the lines, and learning capital letters. Many children don't get these skills at home. They need Pre-K to prepare them for kindergarten.

The minuses of Pre-K are not as obvious, but they are real. Children at this young age need the comfort of home. They need to spend time with parents, not strangers. They need that security. If parents are able to, they can give children the background they need to do well in school.

Other minuses include the fact that a lot of four year-old children can't handle school. They don't have the maturaty to sit still, pay attention, or share with others. Given another year, they may mature enough to do just fine in school. Sometimes it's better just to wait.

So there are definitely good things about Pre-K programs in our public schools, and I would definitely want to see one in our local schools. However, I think parents should decide whether their children are ready for a Pre-K education or not.

Evaluation of Sample Score 3-4 Essay
This paper has an identifiable organization plan, with pros and cons listed in order. The development is easy to understand, if not somewhat simplistic. The language of the paper is uneven, with some vague turns of phrase: "Just like everything in life," "definitely some good things." The word "maturity" is also misspelled. However, the essay is clear and controlled, and generally follows written conventions. If the writer had included more developed and explicit examples and used more varied words, this paper might have earned a higher score.

Sample Score 1-2 Essay
Is early childhood education a good idea? It depends on the child you're talking about. Some children probally need more education in the early years and need something to do to keep out of trouble. Like if there isnt any good nursry school or day care around it could be very good to have Pre-Kindergarten at the school so those children could have a good start on life. A lot of skills could be learned in Pre-Kindergarten, for example they could learn to write their name, cut paper, do art, etc.

Of course theres some kids who wouldnt do well, acting out and so on, so they might do better staying home than going to Pre-Kindergarten, because they just arent ready for school, and maybe wouldn't even be ready for kindergarten the next year either. Some kids just act younger than others or are too baby-ish for school.

So I would suport Pre-Kindergarten in our schools, it seems like a good idea to have someplace for those kids to go. Even if some kids wouldnt do well I think enough kids would do well, and it would make a diference in their grades as they got older. All those skills that they learned would help them in the future. If we did have Pre-Kindergarten it would help their working parents too, knowing their kids were someplace safe and learning importent things for life.

Evaluation of Sample Score 1-2 Essay

Although the writer of this paper has some good points to make, a lack of language skills, considerable misspellings, and a certain disconnectedness of thought keep the paper from scoring high. The paper begins with a vague introduction of the topic and ends with a paragraph that expresses the author's opinion, but the rest of the paper is disorganized. The reasons given do not always have examples to support them, and the examples that are given are weak.

Sample Score 1 Essay

What are benefits? What are some of problems with sending four-year-olds to school? Well, for one problem, its hard to see how little kids would do with all those big kids around at the school. They might get bullyed or lern bad habits, so I wouldnt want my four year old around those big kids on the bus and so on. Its hard to see how that could be good for a four year old. In our area we do have Pre-Kindergarten at our school but you dont have to go there a lot of kids in the program, I think about 50 or more, you see them a lot on the play ground mostly all you see them do is play around so its hard to see how that could be too usefull. They could play around at home just as easy. A reason for not doing Pre-Kindergarten is then what do you learn in Kindergarten. Why go do the same thing two years when you could just do one year when your a little bit bigger (older). I wonder do the people who want Pre-Kindergarten just want there kids out of the house or a baby sitter for there kids. Its hard to see why do we have to pay for that. I dont even know if Kindergarten is so usefull anyway, not like first grade where you actually learn something. So I would say theres lots of problems with Pre-Kindergarten.

Evaluation of Sample Score 1 Essay

This paper barely responds to the prompt. It gives reasons not to support Pre-K instruction, but it does not present any benefits of starting school early. The writer repeats certain phrases ("It's hard to see") to no real effect, and the faulty spelling, grammar, and punctuation significantly impede understanding. Several sentences wander off the topic entirely ("there a lot of kids in the program, I think about 50 or more, you see them a lot on the playground.", "I dont even know if Kindergarten is so usefull anyway, not like first grade where you actually learn something."). Instead of opening with an introduction, the writer simply lifts phrases from the prompt. The conclusion states the writer's opinion, but the reasons behind it are illogical and vague. Rather than organizing the essay in paragraph form, the writer has written a single, run-on paragraph. The lack of organization, weak language skills, and failure to address the prompt earn this essay a 2.

Chapter 4: Mathematics Review

Test Your Knowledge: Mathematics Question Bank

Test Your Knowledge: Percent/Part/Whole, Percent Change

1. In a class of 42 students, 18 are boys. Two girls get transferred to another school. What percent of students remaining are girls?
   a) 14%.
   b) 16%.
   c) 52.4%.
   d) 60%.
   e) None of the above.

2. A payroll check is issued for $500.00. If 20% goes to bills, 30% of the remainder goes to pay entertainment expenses, and 10% of what is left is placed in a retirement account, then approximately how much is remaining?
   a) $150.
   b) $250.
   c) $170.
   d) $350.
   e) $180.

3. A painting by Van Gogh increased in value by 80% from year 1995 to year 2000. If in year 2000, the painting is worth $7200, what was its value in 1995?
   a) $1500.
   b) $2500.
   c) $3000.
   d) $4000.
   e) $5000.

4. "Dresses and Ties" sells a particular dress for $60 dollars. But, they decide to discount the price of that dress by 25%. How much does the dress cost now?
   a) $55.
   b) $43.
   c) $45.
   d) $48.
   e) $65.

5. A sweater goes on sale for 30% off. If the original price was $70, what is the discounted price?
   a) $48.
   b) $49.
   c) $51.
   d) $65.
   e) $52.

6. If the value of a car depreciates by 60% over ten years, and its value in the year 2000 is $2500, what was its value in the year 1990?
   a) $6000.
   b) $6230.
   c) $6250.
   d) $6500.
   e) $6600.

7. If an account is opened with a starting balance of $500, what is the amount in the account after 3 years if the account pays compound interest of 5%?
    a) $560.80.
    b) $578.81.
    c) $564.50.
    d) $655.10.
    e) $660.00.

8. A piece of memorabilia depreciates by 1% every year. If the value of the memorabilia is $75000, what will it be 2 years from now? Give the answer as a whole number.
    a) $74149.
    b) $74150.
    c) $73151.
    d) $71662.
    e) $73507.

9. A dress is marked down by 20% in an effort to boost sales for one week. After that week, the price of the dress is brought back to the original value. What percent did the price of the dress have to be increased from its discounted price?
    a) 20%.
    b) 25%.
    c) 120%.
    d) 125%.
    e) 15%.

10. A car dealer increases the price of a car by 30%, but then discounts it by 30%. What is the relationship between the final price and the original price?
    a) $.91x : x$.
    b) $.98x : x$.
    c) $1:1$.
    d) $.88x : x$.
    e) $.75x : x$.

Test Your Knowledge: Percent/Part/Whole, Percent – Answers

1. e)

The entire class has 42 students, 18 of which are boys, meaning 42 - 18 = 24 is the number of girls. Out of these 24 girls, 2 leave; so 22 girls are left. The total number of students is now 42 - 2 = 40.

22/40 * 100 = 55%.

Reminder: If you forget to subtract 2 from the total number of students, you will end up with 60% as the answer. Sometimes you may calculate an answer that has been given as a choice; it can still be incorrect. Always check your answer.

2. b)

If out of the entire paycheck, 20% is first taken out, then the remainder is 80%. Of this remainder, if 30% is used for entertainment, then (.8 - .80 * .30) = .560 is left. If 10% is put into a retirement account, then (.56 - .56 * .1) = .504 is remaining. So out of $500, the part that remains is 50%, which is $252.

3. d)

In 2005, the value was 1.8 times its value in 1995. So $1.8x = 7200 \rightarrow x = 4000$.

4. c)

60 * (100 - 25)/100 $\rightarrow$ 60 * .75 = 45.

5. b)

New price = original price * (1 – discount) $\rightarrow$ new price = 70(1-.3) = 49.

6. c)

$Value_{2000}$ = Original price * (1-.6) $\rightarrow$ 2500 = .4P = 2500 $\rightarrow$ P = 6250.

7. b)

Amount = $P(1 + r)^t$ = 500 * 1.05^3 = $578.81.

8. e)

Final value = 75000$(1 - .1)^2$ = 73507.

9. b)

If the original price of the dress was x, then the discounted price would be $0.8x$. To increase the price from $.8x$ to x, the percent increase would be $(x - .8x)/.8x$ * 100 = 25%.

10. a)

Let the original price of the car be x. After the 30% increase, the price is $1.3x$.

After discounting the increased price by 30%, it now is $.7 * 1.3x = .91x$. Therefore, the ratio of the final price to the original price $= .91x : x$.

Test Your Knowledge: Mean, Median, Mode

1. If test A is taken 5 times with an average result of 21, and test B is taken 13 times with an average result of 23, what is the combined average?
    a) 22.24.
    b) 22.22.
    c) 22.00.
    d) 22.44.
    e) 24.22.

2. A set of data has 12 entries. The average of the first 6 entries is 12, the average of the next two entries is 20, and the average of the remaining entries is 4. What is the average of the entire data set?
    a) 10.
    b) 10.67.
    c) 11.
    d) 12.67.
    e) 10.5.

3. What is the average score of 8 tests where the score for 3 tests is 55, the score for two tests is 35, and the remaining tests have scores of 70?
    a) 50.3.
    b) 52.5.
    c) 55.1.
    d) 56.0.
    e) 55.6.

4. The temperatures over a week are recorded as follows:

Day	High	Low
Monday	80	45
Tuesday	95	34
Wednesday	78	47
Thursday	79	55
Friday	94	35
Saturday	67	46
Sunday	76	54

    What is the approximate average high temperature and average low temperature during the week?
    a) 90, 50.
    b) 80, 40.
    c) 81, 45.
    d) 82, 46.
    e) 81, 47.

5. Twelve teams competed in a mathematics test. The scores recorded for each team are: 29, 30, 28, 27, 35, 43, 45, 50, 46, 37, 44, and 41. What is the median score?
   a) 37.
   b) 41.
   c) 39.
   d) 44.
   e) 45.

6. A class of 10 students scores 90, 78, 45, 98, 84, 79, 66, 87, 78, and 94. What is the mean score? What is the median score? What is the mode?
   a) 69.9, 81.5, 78.
   b) 79.9, 80, 78.
   c) 79.9, 87, 76.
   d) Not enough information given.
   e) None of the above.

7. A shop sells 3 kinds of t-shirts: one design sells for $4.50, the second for $13.25, and the third for $15.50. If the shop sold 8 shirts of the first design, 12 shirts of the second design, and 4 shirts of the third design, what was the average selling price of the shirts?
   a) $10.71.
   b) $10.25.
   c) $14.55.
   d) $12.55.
   e) $5.80.

Test Your Knowledge: Mean, Median, Mode – Answers

1. **d)**
   If test A avg = 21 for 5 tests, then sum of test A results = 21 * 5 = 105.
   If test B avg = 23 for 13 tests, then sum of test B results = 23 * 13 = 299.
   So total result = 299 + 105 = 404.
   Average of all tests = 404/(5 + 13) = 404/18 = 22.44.

2. **b)**
   The average of the first 6 points is 12 → $s_1/6 = 12$ → $s_1 = 72$; s_1 is the sum of the first 6 points.

   The average of the next 2 points is 20 → $s_2/2 = 20$ → $s_2 = 40$; s_2 is the sum of the next 2 points.

   The average of the remaining 4 points is 4 → $s_3/4 = 4$ → $s_3 = 16$; s_3 is the sum of the last 4 points.

   The sum of all the data points = 72 + 40 + 16 = 128.

   The average = 128/12 = 10.67.

3. **e)**
   Average = (3 * 55 + 2 * 35 + 3 * 70)/8 → Average = 55.625.

4. **c)**
   Average of high s = (80 + 95 + 78 + 79 + 94 + 67 + 76)/7 = 81.29.

   Average of low s = (45 + 34 + 47 + 55 + 35 + 46 + 54)/7 = 45.14.

5. **c)**
   To find the median, we first have to put the list in order:

   27, 28, 29, 30, 35, 37, 41, 43, 44, 45, 46, 50.

   The middle two scores are 37 and 41, and their average is 39.

6. **e) None of the above**
   The mean is just the total score/number of scores → 90 +... + 94)/10 → 79.9.

   The median is the score located in the middle. The middle of the set of the numbers is between 84 and 79. The average of these two scores is 81.5.

   The mode is the number that occurs the most: 78.

7. **a)**
   Multiply each t-shirt price with the number sold; add them together and divide by the total number of shirts sold.

   So Average Price = (4.50 * 8 + 13.25 * 12 + 15.50 * 4)/(8 + 12 + 4) → $10.71.

Test Your Knowledge: Exponents and Roots

1. What is $x^2y^3z^5/y^2z^{-9}$?
   a) y^5z^4.
   b) yz^4.
   c) x^2yz^{14}.
   d) $x^2y^5z^4$.
   e) xyz.

2. What is k if $(2m^3)^5 = 32m^{k+1}$?
   a) 11.
   b) 12.
   c) 13.
   d) 14.
   e) 15.

3. What is $x^5y^4z^3/x^{-3}y^2z^{-4}$?
   a) $x^6y^4z^7$.
   b) x^8yz^7.
   c) x^6yz^7.
   d) $x^8y^2z^7$.
   e) $x^6y^2z^7$.

4. Evaluate $(a^2 * a^{54} + a^{56} + (a^{58}/a^2))/a^4$.
   a) a^{56}.
   b) $3a^{56}$.
   c) $3a^{52}$.
   d) $3a^{54}$.
   e) a^{54}.

5. $9^m = 3^{-1/n}$. What is mn?
   a) .5.
   b) 2.
   c) -2.
   d) -.5.
   e) -1.

6. If $2^a*4^a = 32$, what is a?
   a) 1/3.
   b) 2/3.
   c) 1.
   d) 4/3.
   e) 5/3.

Test Your Knowledge: Exponents and Roots – Answers

1. **c)**
   $x^2y^3z^5/y^2z^{-9} = x^2y^3z^5 * y^{-2}z^9$ which gives the answer $x^2y^{(3-2)}z^{(5+9)} \rightarrow x^2yz^{14}$.

2. **d)**
   Expand $(2m^3)^5$ to give $32m^{15}$.

   So $32m^{15} = 32m^{k+1} \rightarrow k+1 = 15 \rightarrow k = 14$.

3. **d)**
   $x^5y^4z^3/x^{-3}y^2z^{-4} = x^5y^4z^3 * x^3y^{-2}z^4 = x^8y^2z^7$.

4. **c)**
   $(a^2*a^{54}+a^{56}+ (a^{58}/a^2))/a^4 = (a^{54}+2+a^{56}+a^{58}-2)a^{-4} = 3a^{56}-4 = 3a^{52}$.

5. **d)**
   9^m is the same as 3^{2m}.

   So $3^{2m} = 3^{-1/n} \rightarrow 2m = -1/n \rightarrow mn = -.5$.

6. **e)**
   $2^a * 4^a$ can be re-written as $2^a * (2^2)^a$.

   $32 = 2^5$.

   Therefore, $2^{(a+2a)} = 2^5 \rightarrow 3a = 5 \rightarrow a = 5/3$.

Test Your Knowledge: Algebraic Equations

1. The number $568cd$ should be divisible by 2, 5, and 7. What are the values of the digits c and d?
   a) 56835.
   b) 56830.
   c) 56860.
   d) 56840.
   e) 56800.

2. Carla is 3 times older than her sister Megan. Eight years ago, Carla was 18 years older than her sister. What is Megan's age?
   a) 10.
   b) 8.
   c) 9.
   d) 6.
   e) 5.

3. What is the value of $f(x) = (x^2 - 25)/(x + 5)$ when $x = 0$?
   a) -1.
   b) -2.
   c) -3.
   d) -4.
   e) -5.

4. Four years from now, John will be twice as old as Sally will be. If Sally was 10 eight years ago, how old is John?
   a) 35.
   b) 40.
   c) 45.
   d) 50.
   e) 55.

5. I have some marbles. I give 25% to Vic, 20% to Robbie, 10% to Jules. I then give 6/20 of the remaining amount to my brother, and keep the rest for myself. If I end up with 315 marbles, how many did I have to begin with?
   a) 1000.
   b) 1500.
   c) 3500.
   d) 400.
   e) 500.

6. I have some marbles. I give 25% to Vic, 20% of the remainder to Robbie, 10% of that remainder to Jules and myself I then give 6/20 of the remaining amount to my brother, and keep the rest for myself. If I end up with 315 marbles, how many did I have to begin with?
   a) 800.
   b) 833.
   c) 834.
   d) 378.
   e) 500.

7. If $x = 5y + 4$, what is the value of y if $x = 29$?
    a) 33/5.
    b) 5.5.
    c) 5.
    d) 0.
    e) 29/5.

8. A bag of marbles has 8 marbles. If I buy 2 bags of marbles, how many more bags of marbles would I need to buy to have a total of at least 45 marbles?
    a) 3.
    b) 4.
    c) 5.
    d) 6.
    e) 29.

9. A factory that produces widgets wants to sell them each for $550. It costs $50 for the raw materials for each widget, and the startup cost for the factory was $10000. How many widgets have to be sold so that the factory can break even?
    a) 10.
    b) 20.
    c) 30.
    d) 40.
    e) 50.

10. Expand $(3x - 4)(6 - 2x)$.
    a) $6x^2 - 6x + 8$.
    b) $-6x^2 + 26x - 24$.
    c) $6x^2 - 26x + 24$.
    d) $-6x^2 + 26x + 24$.
    e) $6x^2 + 26x - 24$.

11. If $6n + m$ is divisible by 3 and 5, which of the following numbers when added to $6n + m$ will still give a result that is divisible by 3 and 5?
    a) 4.
    b) 6.
    c) 12.
    d) 20.
    e) 60.

12. If x is negative, and $x^3/5$ and $x/5$ both give the same result, what could be the value of x?
    a) -5.
    b) -4.
    c) 3.
    d) 0.
    e) -1.

13. If $m = 3548$, and $n = 235$, then what is the value of $m * n$?
   a) 87940.
   b) 843499.
   c) 87900.
   d) 8830.
   e) 833780.

14. A ball is thrown at a speed of 30 mph. How far will it travel in 2 minutes and 35 seconds?
   a) 1.5 miles.
   b) 1.20 miles.
   c) 1.29 miles.
   d) 1.3 miles.
   e) 1.1 miles.

15. Simplify: $30(\sqrt{40} - \sqrt{60})$.
   a) $30(\sqrt{5} - \sqrt{15})$.
   b) $30(\sqrt{10} + \sqrt{15})$.
   c) $60(\sqrt{5} + \sqrt{15})$.
   d) $60(\sqrt{10} - \sqrt{15})$.
   e) 60.

16. Simplify: $30/(\sqrt{40} - \sqrt{60})$.
   a) $3(\sqrt{5} + \sqrt{15})$.
   b) $-3(\sqrt{5} - \sqrt{15})$.
   c) $-3(\sqrt{10} + \sqrt{15})$.
   d) $3(\sqrt{10} + \sqrt{15})$.
   e) $3(\sqrt{10} - \sqrt{15})$.

17. What is the least common multiple of 2, 3, 4, and 5?
   a) 30.
   b) 60.
   c) 120.
   d) 40.
   e) 50.

18. It costs $6 to make a pen that sells for $12. How many pens need to be sold to make a profit of $60?
   a) 10.
   b) 6.
   c) 72.
   d) 30.
   e) 12.

Test Your Knowledge: Algebraic Equations – Answers

1. **d)**

   If the number is divisible by 2, d should be even. If the number is divisible by 5, then b has to equal 0.

   Start by making both variables 0 and dividing by the largest factor, 7.

   56800/7 = 8114.

   2 from 56800 is 56798, a number divisible by 2 and 7.

   Next add a multiple of 7 that turns the last number to a 0. 6 * 7 = 42. 56798 + 42 = 56840, which is divisible by 2, 5, and 7.

2. **c)**

   Carla's age is c; Megan's age is m. $c = 3m$; $c - 8 = m - 8 + 18$.

   Substitute $3m$ for c in equation 2 → $3m - 8 = m + 10$ → $m = 9$.

3. **e)**

   We know $(x^2 - 25) = (x + 5)(x - 5)$.

   So $(x^2 - 25)/(x + 5) = x - 5$. At $x = 0$, $f(0) = -5$.

4. **b)**

   Let j be John's age and s be Sally's age.

   $j + 4 = 2(s + 4)$.

   $s - 8 = 10$ → $s = 18$.

   So $j + 4 = 2(18 + 4)$ → $j = 40$.

5. **a)**

   If x is the number of marbles initially, then $.25x$ goes to Vic, $.2x$ goes to Robbie, and $.1x$ goes to Jules.

   The number left, x, is $(1 - .25 - .2 - .1) = .45x$.

   Of that I give 6/20 to my brother, so $6/20 * .45x$.

   I am left with $.45x(1 - (6/20)) = .315x$.

   We are also told $.315x = 315$ → $x = 1000$.

6. **c)**

   Always read the question carefully! Questions 5 and 6 are similar, but they are not the same.

Let x be the original number of marbles. After Vic's share is given $.75x$ remains. After Robbie's share $.75x * .80$ remains. After Jules' share, $.75x * .8 * .9$ remains.

After I give my brother his share, $.75x * .8 * .9 * (1 - 6/20)$ remains. The remaining number $= .378x$.

We are told $.378x = 315 \rightarrow x = 833.33$. We need to increase this to the next highest number, 834, because we have part of a marble and to include it we need to have a whole marble.

7. c)

Replace the value of x with its value and solve the equation.

$29 = 5y + 4$.

Solving:

$29 - 4 = 5y + 4 - 4$.

$25 = 5y$ or $5y = 25$.

$5y/5 = 25/5$.

$y = 5$.

8. b)

$2(8) + x > 45$ means $x > 29$, so we need more than 29 marbles. A bag has 8 marbles, so the number of bags needed is 29/8, or 3.625. Since we need 3 bags + part of another bag, we need 4 additional bags to give at least 45 marbles.

9. b)

n is the number of widgets. The cost the factory incurs for making n widgets is $10000 + 50n$. The amount the factory makes by selling n widgets is $550n$.

At the break-even point, the cost incurred is equal to the amount of sales.

$10000 + 50n = 550n \rightarrow n = 20$.

10. b)

Use FOIL:

$(3x - 4)(6 - 2x) = 3x * 6 - 4 * 6 + 3x * (-2x) - 4 * (-2x) = 18x - 24 - 6x^2 + 8x = -6x^2 + 26x - 24$.

11. e)

Since $6n + m$ is divisible by 3 and 5, the new number that we get after adding a value will be divisible by 3 and 5 only if the value that we add is divisible by 3 and 5. The only number that will work from the given choices is 60.

12. e)

We are told $x^3/5 = x/5 \rightarrow x^3 = x$. The possible values are -1, 0, and 1. We are told that x is negative.

So $x = -1$.

13. e)

This problem can be done by elimination. We know that m is in the thousands, which means $x * 10^3$; and n is in the hundreds, which is $y * 10^2$. The answer will be $z * 10^5$, or 6 places in total, so we can eliminate **a)**, **c)**, and **d)**. Also we see that m ends in 8 and n ends in 5, so the answer has to end in 0 ($8 * 5 = 40$), which eliminates **b)**.

14. c)

The ball has a speed of 30 miles per hour. 30 miles per 60 minutes = .5 mile per minute; 2 minutes and 35 seconds = 2 minutes; and 35/60 minutes = 2.58 minutes.

The ball travels .5 * 2.58 = 1.29 miles.

15. d)

$$30\left(\sqrt{40} - \sqrt{60}\right) = 30\sqrt{4\,(10 - 15)} = 60(\sqrt{10} - \sqrt{15}).$$

16. c)

Multiply the numerator and the denominator by $\left(\sqrt{40} + \sqrt{60}\right)$.

So $\dfrac{30}{\left(\sqrt{40}-\sqrt{60}\right)} * \left[\dfrac{\left(\sqrt{40}+\sqrt{60}\right)}{\left(\sqrt{40}+\sqrt{60}\right)}\right] =$

$30\left(\sqrt{40} + \sqrt{60}\right)/\left(\sqrt{40} - \sqrt{60}\right)^2.$

$-3\left(\sqrt{10} + \sqrt{15}\right).$

17. b)

Find all the prime numbers that multiply to give the numbers.

For 2, prime factor is 2; for 3, prime factor is 3; for 4, prime factors are 2, 2; and for 5, prime factor is 5. Note the maximum times of occurrence of each prime and multiply these to find the least common multiple.

The LCM is 2 * 2 * 3 * 5 = 60.

18. a)

One pen sells for $12, so on the sale of a pen, the profit is 12 - 6 = 6.

In order to make $60, we need to sell 10 pens.

Test Your Knowledge: Inequalities, Literal Equations, Polynomials, and Binomials

1. If $x < 5$ and $y < 6$, then $x + y \underline{\ ?\ } 11$.
   a) $<$
   b) $>$
   c) $\leq$
   d) $\geq$
   e) $=$

2. Which of the following is true about the inequality $25x^2 - 40x - 32 < 22$?
   a) There are no solutions.
   b) There is a set of solutions.
   c) There is 1 solution only.
   d) There are 2 solutions.
   e) There are 3 solutions.

3. If $x - 2y > 6$, what possible values of y always have x as greater than or equal to 2?
   a) $y \geq 1$.
   b) $y \leq 0$.
   c) $y \geq -2$.
   d) $y < 2$.
   e) $y \leq 6$.

4. Find the point of intersection of the lines $x + 2y = 4$ and $3x - y = 26$.
   a) $(1, 3)$.
   b) $(8, -2)$.
   c) $(0, 2)$.
   d) $(2, -1)$.
   e) $(4, 26)$.

5. If $a + b = 2$, and $a - b = 4$, what is a?
   a) 1.
   b) 2.
   c) 3.
   d) 4.
   e) 5.

6. If $\sqrt{a} + \sqrt{b} = 2$, and $\sqrt{a} - \sqrt{b} = 3$, what is $a + b$?
   a) 6.5.
   b) 6.
   c) 5.5.
   d) 5.
   e) 4.5.

7. If $a = b + 3$, and $3b = 5a + 6$, what is $3a - 2b$?
   a) -1.5.
   b) 2.5.
   c) 3.
   d) 4.3.
   e) 5.

8. The sum of the roots of a quadratic equation is 8, and the difference is 2. What is the equation?
   a) $x^2 - 8x - 15$.
   b) $x^2 + 8x + 15$.
   c) $x^2 - 8x + 15$.
   d) $x^2 + 8x - 15$.
   e) $x^2 + 15$.

9. Solve the following system of equations: $3x + 2y = 7$ and $3x + y = 5$.
   a) $x = 2, y = 1$.
   b) $x = 2, y = 2$.
   c) $x = 1, y = 0$.
   d) $x = 1, y = 2$.
   e) $x = 1, y = 1$.

10. Nine tickets were sold for $41. If the tickets cost $4 and $5, how many $5 tickets were sold?
    a) 5.
    b) 4.
    c) 9.
    d) 6.
    e) 7.

11. Joe brought a bag of 140 M&Ms to his class of 40 students. Each boy received 2 M&Ms. Each girl received 4. How many boys were in the class?
    a) 10.
    b) 20.
    c) 30.
    d) 40.
    e) 50.

Test Your Knowledge: Inequalities, Literal Equations, Polynomials, and Binomials – Answers

1. **a)**
   Choice **a)** will always be true, while the other choices can never be true.

2. **b)**
   $25x^2 - 40x + 32 < 22 \rightarrow 25x^2 - 40x + 16 < 6 \rightarrow (5x - 4)^2 < 6 \rightarrow 5x - 4 < 6$.

   $x = 2$, so x has to be all numbers less than 2 for this inequality to work.

3. **c)**
   Rearrange equation $x > 6 + 2y$, so $2 > 6 + 2y$. Solve for y.

   $2 \geq 6 + 2y$.

   $-4 \geq 2y$, so $-2 \leq y$ or $y \geq -2$.

   (When working with inequalities, remember to reverse the sign when dividing by a negative number.)

4. **b)**
   Find the slopes first. If they are not equal, then the lines intersect. The slopes are -1/2 and 3.

   Next, solve by substitution or addition. From the first equation, $x = 4 - 2y$. Plugging this into equation 2, we get $3(4 - 2y) - y = 26 \rightarrow 7y = 12 - 26 \rightarrow y = -2$. Plug this value into either equation to find x.

   With equation 1, we get $x - 4 = 4 \rightarrow x = 8$.

5. **c)**
   Add the equations to eliminate b. $2a = 6 \rightarrow a = 3$.

6. **a)**
   Square both equations.

   Equation 1 becomes $a + 2\sqrt{ab} + b = 4$; and equation 2 becomes $a - 2\sqrt{ab} + b = 9$.

   Add the equations.
   $2(a + b) = 13 \rightarrow a + b = 13/2$. $13/2 = 6.5$.

7. **a)**
   Solve by substitution.

   If $a = b + 3$, and $3b = 5a + 6$, then $3b = 5(b+3) + 6$.

   If $3b - 5b - 15 = 6$, then $-2b = 21$. Therefore, $b = -10.5$.

   Now use substitution to find a.

$a = b + 3$. So $a = -10.5 + 3$. Therefore, $a = -7.5$.

Solve the equation, $3a - 2b$.

$3(-7.5) - 2(-10.5) = -1.5$.

8. **c)**

   If the roots are a and b, then $a + b = 8$ and $a - b = 2$.

   Add the equations. $2a = 10 \rightarrow a = 5 \rightarrow b = 3$.

   The factors are $(x - 5)(x - 3)$, and the equation is $x^2 - 8x + 15$.

9. **d)**

   From the equation $3x + y = 5$, we get $y = 5 - 3x$. Substitute into the other equation. $3x + 2(5 - 3x) = 7$ $\rightarrow 3x + 10 - 6x = 7 \rightarrow x = 1$. This value into either of the equations gives us $y = 2$.

10. **a)**

    $4x + 5y = 41$, and $x + y = 9$, where x and y are the number of tickets sold.

    From equation 2: $x = 9 - y$.

    From equation 1: $4(9 - y) + 5y = 41 \rightarrow 36 + y = 41 \rightarrow y = 5$.

11. **a)**

    b is the number of boys, and g is the number of girls. So $b + g - 40$, and $2b + 4g = 140$.

    To do the problem, use the substitution method. Plug $(g = 40 - b)$ into $(2b + 4g = 140)$.

    $2b + 4(40 - b) = 140 \rightarrow b = 10$.

Test Your Knowledge: Slope and Distance to Midpoint

1. What is the equation of the line that passes through (3, 5), with intercept $y = 8$?
   a) $y = x + 8$.
   b) $y = x - 8$.
   c) $y = -x - 8$.
   d) $y = -x + 8$.
   e) $y = -x$.

2. What is the value of y in the equation $(3x - 4)^2 = 4y - 15$, if $x = 3$?
   a) 10.
   b) 2.5.
   c) -10.
   d) -2.5.
   e) 5.

3. If $y = 4x + 6y$, what is the range of y if $-10 < x \leq 5$?
   a) $-4 < y \leq 8$.
   b) $-4 < y < 8$.
   c) $8 > y > -4$.
   d) $-4 \leq y < 8$.
   e) $-4 \leq y \leq 8$.

4. If Jennifer gets three times as much allowance as Judy gets, and Judy gets $5/week, how much does Jennifer get every month?
   a) $15.
   b) $20.
   c) $30.
   d) $45.
   e) $60.

5. What is the value of x, if $y = 8$ in the equation $5x + 9y = 3x - 6y + 5$?
   a) 57.5.
   b) 60.
   c) -60.
   d) -57.5.
   e) None of the above.

6.

A (3, 5)   B (8, 17)

What is the area outside the circle, but within the square whose two corners are A and B?
   a) 169(1-π).
   b) 169 π.
   c) 169 π /4.
   d) 169(1- π /4).
   e) 169.

7. A line with a slope of 2 passes through the point (2, 4). What is the set of coordinates where that line passes through the y intercept?
   a) (-2, 0).
   b) (0, 0).
   c) (2, 2).
   d) (4, 0).
   e) (1, 1).

8.

$$3x + 4y = 7$$
$$9x + 12y = 21$$

Determine where the above two lines intersect:
   a) $x = 4, y = 3$.
   b) $x = 12, y = 9$.
   c) $x = 1/3, y = 1/3$.
   d) Not enough information provided.
   e) There is no solution; the lines do not intersect.

9.

$$3x + 4y = 7$$
$$8x - 6y = 9$$

Are the above lines parallel or perpendicular?
   a) Parallel.
   b) Perpendicular.
   c) Neither parallel nor perpendicular.
   d) Cannot be determined.
   e) The angle at the point of intersection is 40.

10. Is the graph of the function $f(x) = -3x^2 + 4$ linear, asymptotical, symmetrical to the x axis, symmetrical to the y axis, or not symmetrical to either axis?

    a) Symmetrical to the x axis.
    b) Symmetrical to the y axis.
    c) Symmetrical to neither axis.
    d) Asymptotic.
    e) Linear.

11. Two points on a line have coordinates (3, 12) and (9, 20). What is the distance between these two points?

    a) 10.
    b) 12.
    c) 13.
    d) 8.
    e) 11.

12. In the following graph, what is the equation of line AB if line AB is perpendicular to line PQ? Point coordinates are:

M (-4, 0); O (0, 2); and N (0, -3). The lines intersect at (-2,1).

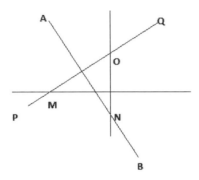

    a) $y = 2x + 3$.
    b) $y = -2x - 3$.
    c) $y = x - 4$.
    d) $y = x + 3$.
    e) $y = -2x - 3$.

13. What is the equation of a line passing through (1, 2) and (6, 12)?

    a) $y = x$.
    b) $y = 2x$.
    c) $y = x/2$.
    d) $y = 2x + 2$.
    e) $y = x - 2$.

14. What is the midpoint of the line connecting points (0, 8) and (2, 6)?

    a) (-1, 1).
    b) (2, 14).
    c) (-2, 2).
    d) (0, 1).
    e) (1, 7).

15. What is the equation of a line passing through (1, 1) and (2, 4)?
   a) $3y = x + 2$.
   b) $2y = x + 3$.
   c) $y = 3x - 2$.
   d) $4x = y + 2$.
   e) $y = (1/3)x + 2$.

16. Line A passes through (0, 0) and (3, 4). Line B passes through (2, 6) and (3, y). What value of y will make the lines parallel?
   a) 20/3.
   b) 7.
   c) 22/3.
   d) 29.
   e) 5.

17. Line A passes through (1, 3) and (3, 4). Line B passes through (3, 7) and (5, y). What value of y will make the lines perpendicular?
   a) 1.
   b) 2.
   c) 3.
   d) 4.
   e) 5.

18. What is the equation of line A that is perpendicular to line B, connecting (8, 1) and   (10, 5), that intersects at (x, 14)?
   a) $y = 2x - 7$.
   b) $y = -2x + 7$.
   c) $y = (-1/2)x + 19\frac{1}{4}$.
   d) $y = 5x - 7$.
   e) $y = 2x - 19\frac{1}{4}$.

Test Your Knowledge: Slope and Distance to Midpoint – Answers

1. **d)**

   The standard form of the line equation is $y = mx + b$. We need to find slope m.

   $m = (y_2 - y_1)/(x_2 - x_1)$ → $m = (5 - 8)/(3 - 0)$ → $m = -1$.

   Therefore the equation is $y = -x + 8$.

2. **a)**

   At $x = 3$, $((3 * 3) - 4)^2 = 4y - 15$.

   $(9 - 4)^2 = 4y - 15$.

   $25 = 4y - 15$.

   $40 = 4y$.

   $y = 10$.

3. **d)**

   Rearrange the equation and combine like terms. $-5y = 4x$.

   At $x = -10$, $y = 8$. At $x = 5$, $y = -4$. The range of y is therefore $-4 \leq y < 8$.

4. **e)**

   If Judy gets x dollars, then Jennifer gets $3x$ in a week. In a month, Jennifer will then get $4 * 3x$.

   If Judy gets $5 per week, then Jennifer gets $60 in a month.

5. **d)**

   Combine like terms.

   $5x + 9y = 3x - 6y + 5$ → $2x = -15y + 5$ → $x = -57.5$ when $y = 8$.

6. **d)**

   First we need to find the length of side AB.

   $AB = \sqrt{(17 - 5)^2 + (8 - 3)^2} = 13$.

   If $AB = 13$, then $A_{square} = 13^2 = 169$.

   AB is also the diameter of the circle. $A_{circle} \pi (d^2/4) = 169 \pi /4$.

   The area outside the circle and within the square is: $A_{square} - A_{circle} = 169(1 - \pi /4)$.

7. **b)**

   The slope of the line is given as $m = (y_2 - y_1)/(x_2 - x_1)$, where (x_1, y_1) and (x_2, y_2) are two points which the line passes through.

The y intercept is the point where the graph intersects the y axis, so $x = 0$ at this point.

Plug in the values of m, etc.; we get $2 = (4 - y)/(2 - 0) \rightarrow y = 0$.

8. e)
While it is tempting to solve this system of simultaneous equations to find the values of x and y, the first thing to do is to see whether the lines intersect. To do this, compare the slopes of the two lines by putting the lines into the standard form, $y = mx + b$, where m is the slope.

By rearranging, equation 1 becomes $y = 7/4 - 3x/4$; and equation 2 becomes $y = 21/12 - 9x/12$.

The slope of line 1 is -3/4, and the slope of line 2 is -9/12, which reduces to -3/4. Since the slopes are equal, the lines are parallel and do not intersect.

9. b)
Find the slopes by rearranging the two equations into the form $y = mx + b$.

Equation 1 becomes $y = -3x/4 + 7/4$ and equation 2 becomes $y = 8x/6 - 9/6$.

So $m_1 = -3/4$ and $m_2 = 8/6 = 4/3$. We see that m_1 is the negative inverse of m_2, so line 1 is perpendicular to line 2.

10. b)
Find the values of the y coordinate for different values of the x coordinate (example, [-3, +3]). We get the following chart:

x	y
-3	-23
-2	-8
-1	1
0	4
1	1
2	-8
3	-23

From these values, we see the graph is symmetrical to the y axis.

11. a)
Distance $s = \sqrt{(x_2 - x_1)^2 + (y_2 - y_1)^2} \rightarrow s = \sqrt{(9 - 3)^2 + (20 - 12)^2} = \sqrt{36 + 64} = 10$.

12. b)
$y = mx + b$; m is the slope and b is the y intercept.

Calculate m for line AB using the given points (0, -3) and (-2, 1). $m = (-3 -1)/(0-(-2)) = -2$. The y intercept is -3 (from point set given), so $y = -2x - 3$.
\

13. b)
First, find the slope, $(y_2-y_1)/(x_2-x_1) \rightarrow$ slope $= (12 - 2)/(6 - 1) = 2$.

Next, use the slope and a point to find the value of b.

In the standard line equation, $y = mx + b$, use the point (6, 12) to get $12 = (2 * 6) + b$ → $b = 0$.

The equation of the line is $y = 2x$.

14. e)
The midpoint is at $(x_1 + x_2)/2, (y_1 + y_2)/2 = (1, 7)$.

15. c)
Slope $= (y_2 - y_1)/(x_2 - x_1) = 3$. Plug one of the coordinates into $y = mx + b$ to find the value of b.

$1 = 3(1) + b$ → $b = -2$.

The equation of the line is $y = 3x - 2$.

16. c)
Calculate the slope of each line. Slope of line A $= 4/3$; and slope of line B $= y - 6$.

The slopes of the line have to be the same for the lines to be parallel.

$4/3 = y - 6$ → $4 = 3y - 18$ → $y = 22/3$.

17. c)
The slope of line A $= \frac{1}{2}$; and the slope of line B $= (y - 7)/2$.

The product of the slopes has to equal -1.

$(1/2)[(y - 7)/2] = -1$ → $(y - 7)/4 = -1$ → $y = 3$.

18. c)
$\text{Slope}_b = (5 - 1)/(10 - 8) = 2$. The slope of line A is -1/2.

To find the intercept of line B, use $y = mx + b$.

$5 = (2)(10) + b$, so $b = -7$. Equation of line B is $y = 2x - 7$.

Find intersect x, using the given y coordinate. $14 = 2x - 7; x = 10.5$.

Find the intercept of line A using the coordinates of intersection.

$14 = (-1/2)(10.5) + b. b = 19\frac{1}{4}$.

The equation of line A is $y = -(1/2)x + 19\frac{1}{4}$.

Test Your Knowledge: Absolute Value Equations

1. Factor $x^2 + 2x - 15$.
   a) $(x - 3)(x + 5)$.
   b) $(x + 3)(x - 5)$.
   c) $(x + 3)(x + 5)$.
   d) $(x - 3)(x - 5)$.
   e) $(x - 1)(x + 15)$.

2. Car A starts at 3:15 PM and travels straight to its destination at a constant speed of 50 mph. If it arrives at 4:45 PM, how far did it travel?
   a) 70 miles.
   b) 75 miles.
   c) 65 miles.
   d) 40 miles.
   e) 105 miles.

3. What are the roots of the equation $2x^2 + 14x = 0$?
   a) 0 and 7.
   b) 0 and -7.
   c) 14 and 0.
   d) 2 and 14.
   e) Cannot be determined.

4. If $f(x) = 2x^2 + 3x$, and $g(x) = x + 4$, what is $f[g(x)]$?
   a) $x^2 + 19x + 44$.
   b) $2x^2 + 19x + 44$.
   c) $4x^2 + 35x + 76$.
   d) $x^2 + 8x + 16$.
   e) None of the above.

5. If $|x + 4| = 2$, what are the values of x?
   a) 2 and 6.
   b) -2 and -6.
   c) -2.
   d) -6.
   e) 0.

6. The sale of an item can be written as a function of price: $s = 3p + c$, where s is the amount in sales, p is the price per item, and c is a constant value. If the sales generated are $20 at a price of $5 for the item, then what should the price be to generate $50 in sales?
   a) $10.
   b) $15.
   c) $20.
   d) $16.
   e) $14.

7. If $f(n) = 2n + 3\sqrt{n}$, where n is a positive integer, what is $f[g(5)]$ if $g(m) = m - 4$?
   a) 1.
   b) 2.
   c) 3.
   d) 4.
   e) 5.

8. If $f(x) = (x + 2)^2$, and $-4 \leq x \leq 4$, what is the minimum value of $f(x)$?
   a) 0.
   b) 1.
   c) 2.
   d) 3.
   e) 4.

9. If $f(x) = (x + 2)^2$, and $0 \leq x \leq 4$, what is the minimum value of $f(x)$?
   a) 1.
   b) 2.
   c) 3.
   d) 4.
   e) 5.

10. What is $x^2 - 9$ divided by $x - 3$?
    a) $x - 3$.
    b) $x + 3$.
    c) x.
    d) $x - 1$.
    e) 6.

11. An equation has two roots: 5 and -8. What is a possible equation?
    a) $x^2 - 3x + 40$.
    b) $x^2 - 3x - 40$.
    c) $x^2 + x + 40$.
    d) $x^2 + 3x - 40$.
    e) $2x^2 - 3x + 40$.

12. In an ant farm, the number of ants grows every week according to the formula
    $N = 100 + 2^w$, where w is the number of weeks elapsed. How many ants will the colony have after 5 weeks?
    a) 115.
    b) 125.
    c) 135.
    d) 132.
    e) 233.

13. Find the values of x that validate the following equation: $[(4x + 5)^2 - (40x + 25)]^{1/2} + 3|x| - 14 = 0$.

    a) -2, -14.
    b) 2, -14.
    c) -2, 14.
    d) 2, 14.
    e) No solution.

14. If $|x| = 4$ and $|y| = 5$, what are the values of $|x + y|$?

    a) 1, 9.
    b) -1, 9.
    c) -1, -9.
    d) -1, -9.
    e) $1 < |x + y| < 9$.

15. If $y = |x|$, what is the range of y?

    a) $y < 0$.
    b) $0 < y < x$.
    c) $y > 0$.
    d) $y \geq 0$.
    e) $y > x$.

Test Your Knowledge: Absolute Value Equations – Answers

1. **a)**
   The constant term is -15. The factors should multiply to give -15 and add to give 2.
   The numbers -3 and 5 satisfy both, $(x - 3)(x + 5)$.

2. **b)**
   The time between 3:15 PM and 4:45 PM = 1.5 hours. $1.5 * 50 = 75$.

   Reminder: half an hour is written as .5 of an hour, not .3 of an hour, even though on a clock a half hour is 30 minutes.

3. **b)**
   Rearrange, reduce, and factor.

   $2x^2 + 14x + 0 = 0$.

   $2(x^2 + 7x + 0) = 0$.

   $(x + 7)(x + 0)$.

   $x = 0$, or -7.

4. **b)**
   Substitute $g(x)$ for every x in $f(x)$.

   $f[g((x + 4))] = 2(x + 4)^2 + 3(x + 4) = 2x^2 + 16x + 32 + 3x + 12 = 2x^2 + 19x + 44$.

5. **b)**
   Two solutions: $(x + 4) = 2$ and $-(x + 4) = 2$.

   Or $x + 4 = 2$, $x = -2$.

   And $x + 4 = -2$, $x = -6$.

6. **b)**
   Find the value of the constant by plugging in the given information.

   $20 = 3 * 5 + c \rightarrow c = 5$.

   Now use the value of c and the new value of s to find p. $50 = 3p + 5 \rightarrow p = 15$.

7. **e)**
   $g(5) = 5 - 4 = 1$. $f[g(5)] = 2 * 1 + 3\sqrt{1} = 5$.

8. **a)**
   From the domain of x, the lowest value of x is -4, and the highest value is 4. We are tempted to think that $f(x)$ will have the least value at $x = -4$: $f(-4) = 4$. However, $f(x)$ is equal to a squared value, so the lowest value of $f(x)$ is 0. This happens at $x = -2$.

9. d)

The lowest value of $f(x)$ can be 0, since $f(x)$ is equal to a squared value, but, for $f(x) = 0$, x must equal -2. That is outside the domain of x. The least value of $f(x) = 4$.

10. b)

$x^2 - 9$ can be factored into $(x + 3)$ and $(x - 3)$.

$[(x + 3)(x - 3)]/(x - 3) = x + 3$.

11. d)

If the roots are 5 and -8, then the factors are $(x - 5)(x + 8)$. Multiply the factors to get the equation.

$x^2 + 3x - 40$.

12. d)

After 5 weeks, the number of ants $= 100 + 32$, or 132.

13. d)

Expand the equation:

$[16x^2 + 40x + 25 - 40x - 25]^{1/2} + 3|x| - 14 = 0$.

$(16x^2)^{1/2} + 3|x| - 14 = 0$.

$4x + 3|x| - 14 = 0$.

$3|x| = 14 - 4x$.

$|x| = \dfrac{14}{3} - \dfrac{4x}{3}$ $\qquad x = \dfrac{14}{3} - \dfrac{4x}{3} = 2 \qquad x = -\dfrac{14}{3} - \dfrac{4x}{3} = 14$.

14. a)

$x = 4$ and $y = 5$, $|x + y| = 9$.

$x = -4$ and $y = 5$, $|x + y| = 1$.

$x = 4$ and $y = -5$, $|x + y| = 1$.

$x = -4$ and $y = -5$, $|x + y| = 9$.

15. d)

The absolute value of x can be at least a 0, and is otherwise positive regardless of the value of x.

$y \geq 0$.

Test Your Knowledge: Geometry

1. What is the area, in square feet, of the triangle whose sides have lengths equal to 3, 4, and 5 feet?
   a) 6 square feet.
   b) 7 square feet.
   c) 4 square feet.
   d) 5 square feet.
   e) 8 square feet.

2. In the following figure, where AE bisects line BC, and angles AEC and AEB are both right angles, what is the length of AB?
   a) 1 cm.
   b) 2 cm.
   c) 3 cm.
   d) 4 cm.
   e) 5 cm.

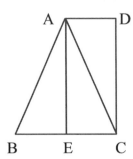

BC = 6 cm
AD = 3 cm
CD = 4 cm

3. In the following triangle, if AB = 6 and BC = 8, what should the length of CA be to make triangle ABC a right triangle?
   a) 10.
   b) 9.
   c) 8.
   d) 4.
   e) 7.

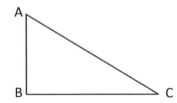

4. In the following circle there is a square with an area of 36 cm². What is the area outside the square, but within the circle?
   a) 18π cm².
   b) 18π - 30 cm².
   c) 18π - 36 cm².
   d) 18 cm².
   e) -18 cm².

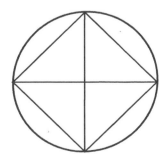

5. The length of a rectangle is 4 times its width. If the width of the rectangle is $5 - x$ inches, and the perimeter of the rectangle is 30 inches, what is x?
  - a) 1.
  - b) 2.
  - c) 3.
  - d) 4.
  - e) 5.

6. Two sides of a triangle have a ratio AC:BC = 5:4. The length of AB on a similar triangle = 24. What is the actual value of AC for the larger triangle?
  - a) 10.
  - b) 14.4.
  - c) 35.
  - d) 40.
  - e) 50.

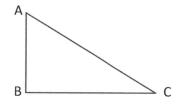

7. If the diameter of a circle is doubled, the area increases by what factor?
  - a) 1 time.
  - b) 2 times.
  - c) 3 times.
  - d) 4 times.
  - e) 5 times.

8. In the following triangle PQR, what is the measure of angle A?
  - a) 145^0.
  - b) 140^0.
  - c) 70^0.
  - d) 50^0.
  - e) 40^0.

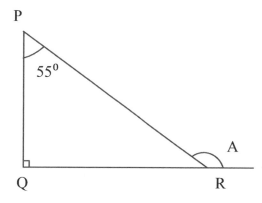

Test Your Knowledge: Geometry – Answers

1. **a)**

   The Pythagorean triple (special right triangle property) means the two shorter sides form a right triangle.

   $1/2bh$ = A. So, $(1/2)(3)(4) = 6$.

2. **e)**

   $AB^2 = AC^2 = AD2 + CD^2 \rightarrow AB^2 = 3^2 + 4^2 \rightarrow AB = 5$.

3. **a)**

   In a right triangle, the square of the hypotenuse = the sum of the squares of the other two sides.

   $AB^2 + BC^2 = AC^2 \rightarrow AC^2 = 36 + 64 \rightarrow AC = 10$.

4. **c)**

   If the area of the square is 36 cm^2, then each side is 6 cm. If we look at the triangle made by half the square, that diagonal would be the hypotenuse of the triangle, and its length = $\sqrt{6^2 + 6^2} = 6\sqrt{2}$.

   This hypotenuse is also the diameter of the circle, so the radius of the circle is $3\sqrt{2}$.

   The area of the circle = $A = \pi r^2 = 18\pi$.

   The area outside the square, but within the circle is 18π -36.

5. **b)**

   Perimeter of a rectangle = $2(l + w)$. Width = $5 - x$; and length = $4(5 - x)$.

   Perimeter = $2(l * w) = 30 \rightarrow 2(20 - 4x + 5 - x) = 30 \rightarrow -10x = -20 \rightarrow x = 2$.

6. **d)**

   Side AC = 5, and side BC = 4. The Pythagorean triple is 3:4:5, so side AB = 3.

   Because the other triangle is similar, the ratio of all sides is constant. AB:AB = 3:24. The ratio factor is 8.

   AC of the larger triangle = 5 * 8 = 40.

7. **d)**

   The area of a circle = πr^2.

   If the diameter is doubled, then the radius is also doubled.

   The new area = $\pi * (2r)^2 = 4 * \pi * r^2$. The area increases four times.

8. **a)**

   $\angle P = 55^0$. $\angle Q = 90^0$. $\angle R = 180 - (55 + 90) = 35^0$, and $\angle A = 180 - 35 = 145^0$.

Test Your Knowledge: Fundamental Counting Principle, Permutations, Combinations

1. The wardrobe of a studio contains 4 hats, 3 suits, 5 shirts, 2 pants, and 3 pairs of shoes. How many different ways can these items be put together?
   a) 60.
   b) 300.
   c) 360.
   d) 420.
   e) 500.

2. For lunch, you have a choice between chicken fingers or cheese sticks for an appetizer; turkey, chicken, or veal for the main course; cake or pudding for dessert; and either Coke or Pepsi for a beverage. How many choices of possible meals do you have?
   a) 16.
   b) 24.
   c) 34.
   d) 36.
   e) 8.

3. For an office job, I need to pick 3 candidates out of a pool of 5. How many choices do I have?
   a) 60.
   b) 20.
   c) 10.
   d) 30.
   e) 50.

4. A contractor is supposed to choose 3 tiles out of a stack of 5 tiles to make as many patterns as possible. How many different patterns can he make?
   a) 10.
   b) 20.
   c) 30.
   d) 40.
   e) 60.

5. I have chores to do around the house on a weekend. There are 5 chores I must complete by the end of the day. I can choose to do them in any order, so long as they are all completed. How many choices do I have?
   a) 5.
   b) 25.
   c) 32.
   d) 3125.
   e) 120.

6. Next weekend, I have more chores to do around the house. There are 5 chores I must complete by the end of the day. I can choose to do any 2 of them in any order, and then do any 2 the next day again in any order, and then do the remaining 1 the following day. How many choices do I have?
    a) 20.
    b) 6.
    c) 120.
    d) 130.
    e) 25.

7. A certain lottery play sheet has 10 numbers from which 5 have to be chosen. How many different ways can I pick the numbers?
    a) 150.
    b) 250.
    c) 252.
    d) 143.
    e) 278.

8. At a buffet, there are 3 choices for an appetizer, 6 choices for a beverage, and 3 choices for an entrée. How many different ways can I select food from all the food choices?
    a) 12.
    b) 27.
    c) 36.
    d) 42.
    e) 54.

9. If there is a basket of 10 assorted fruits, and I want to pick out 3 fruits, how many combinations of fruits do I have to choose from?
    a) 130.
    b) 210.
    c) 310.
    d) 120.
    e) 100.

10. How many ways can I pick 3 numbers from a set of 10 numbers?
    a) 720.
    b) 120.
    c) 180.
    d) 150.
    e) 880.

Test Your Knowledge: Fundamental Counting Principle, Permutations, Combinations – Answers

1. **c)**
   The number of ways = 4 * 3 * 5 * 2 * 3 = 360.

2. **b)**
   Multiply the possible number of choices for each item from which you can choose.

   2 * 3 * 2 * 2 = 24.

3. **c)**
   This is a combination problem. The order of the candidates does not matter.

   The number of combinations = 5!/3!(5 - 3)! = 5 * 4/2 * 1 = 10.

4. **e)**
   This is a permutation problem. The order in which the tiles are arranged is counted.

   The number of patterns = 5!/(5 - 3)! = 5 * 4 * 3 = 60.

5. **e)**
   This is a permutation problem. The order in which the chores are completed matters.

   $^5P_5$ = 5!/(5 - 5)! = 5! = 5 * 4 * 3 * 2 * 1 = 120.

6. **c)**
   #Choices$_{today}$ = $^5P_2$ = 5!/(5 - 2)! = 5 * 4 = 20.

   #Choices$_{tomorrow}$ = $^3P_2$ = 3!/1! = 6.

   #Choices$_{day3}$ = 1.

   The total number of permutations = 20 * 6 * 1 = 120.

7. **c)**
   This is a combinations problem. The order of the numbers is not relevant.

   $^{10}n_5$ = 10!/5!(10 - 5)! = 10 * 9 * 8 * 7 * 6/5 * 4 * 3 * 2 * 1 = 252.

8. **e)**
   There are 3 ways to choose an appetizer, 6 ways to choose a beverage, and 3 ways to choose an entrée. The total number of choices = 3 * 6 * 3 = 54.

9. **d)**
   $^{10}C_3$ = 10!/(3!(10 - 3)!) = 10!/(3! * 7!) = 10 * 9 * 8/3 * 2 * 1 = 120.

10. **b)**
    $^{10}P_4$ = 10!/3!(10 - 3)! = 10 * 9 * 8/3 * 2 * 1 = 120

Test Your Knowledge: Ratios, Proportions, Rate of Change

1. A class has 50% more boys than girls. What is the ratio of boys to girls?
   a) 4:3.
   b) 3:2.
   c) 5:4.
   d) 10:7.
   e) 7:5.

2. A car can travel 30 miles on 4 gallons of gas. If the gas tank has a capacity of 16 gallons, how far can it travel if the tank is ¾ full?
   a) 120 miles.
   b) 90 miles.
   c) 60 miles.
   d) 55 miles.
   e) 65 miles.

3. The profits of a company increase by $5000 every year for five years and then decrease by $2000 for the next two years. What is the average rate of change in the company profit for that seven-year period?
   a) $1000/year.
   b) $2000/year.
   c) $3000/year.
   d) $4000/year.
   e) $5000/year.

4. A bag holds 250 marbles. Of those marbles, 40% are red, 30% are blue, 10% are green, and 20% are black. How many marbles of each color are present in the bag?
   a) Red = 90; Blue = 80; Green = 30; Black = 40.
   b) Red = 80; Blue = 60; Green = 30; Black = 80.
   c) Red = 100; Blue = 75; Green = 25; Black = 50.
   d) Red = 100; Blue = 70; Green = 30; Black = 50.
   e) Red = 120; Blue = 100; Green = 10; Black = 20.

5. Two students from a student body of 30 boys and 50 girls will be selected to serve on the school disciplinary committee. What is the probability that first a boy will be chosen, and then a girl?
   a) 1/1500.
   b) 1500/6400.
   c) 1500/6320.
   d) 1.
   e) 30/50.

6. If number *n*, divided by number *m*, gives a result of .5, what is the relationship between *n* and *m*?

    a) *n* is twice as big as *m*.

    b) *m* is three times as big as *n*.

    c) *n* is a negative number.

    d) *m* is a negative number.

    e) *n* is ½ of *m*.

7. In a fruit basket, there are 10 apples, 5 oranges, 5 pears, and 6 figs. If I select two fruits, what is the probability that I will first pick a pear and then an apple?

    a) .07.

    b) .08.

    c) 1/13.

    d) 13.

    e) 5.

8. In a fruit basket, there are 3 apples, 5 oranges, 2 pears, and 2 figs. If I pick out two fruits, what is the probability that I will pick a fig first and then an apple?
Round to the nearest 100th.

    a) .04.

    b) .05.

    c) .06.

    d) .03.

    e) .02.

9. If *x* workers can make p toys in *c* days, how many toys can y workers make in *d* days if they work at the same rate?

    a) *cp/qx*.

    b) *cq/px*.

    c) *cqy/px*.

    d) *pdy/cx*.

    e) *qy/px*.

10. If a car travels 35 miles on a gallon of gas, how far will it travel on 13 gallons of gas?

    a) 189 miles.

    b) 255 miles.

    c) 335 miles.

    d) 455 miles.

    e) 500 miles.

Test Your Knowledge: Ratios, Proportions, Rate of Change – Answers

1. **b)**
    The ratio of boys to girls is 150:100, or 3:2.

2. **b)**
    A full tank has 16 gallons → 3/4 of the tank = 12 gallons. The car can travel 30 miles on 4 gallons, so 12 gallons would take the car 12 * 30/4 = 90 miles.

3. **c)**
    Average Rate of Change = the change in value/change in time = (total profit – initial profit)/change in time. Initial profit = 0; change in time = 7 years.

    Increase = 5000 * 5 = 25000; decrease = 2000 * 2 = 4000; total profit = 25000 - 4000 = 21000.

    (21000 - 0)/7 years = $3000/year.

4. **c)**
    Total number of marbles = 250.

    #red marbles = 250 * 40/100 = 250 * .4 = 100.

    #blue marbles = 250 * .3 = 75.

    #green marbles = 250 * .1 = 25.

    #black marbles = 250 * .2 = 50.

5. **c)**
    The probability of selecting a boy from the entire group = 30:80.

    The probability of selecting a girl from the remaining group = 50:79.

    The probability of selecting a boy and a girl is (30:80) * (50:79) = 1500:6320.

6. **e)**
    If n/m = .5, then n = .5m, or n = ½ of m.

7. **c)**
    The total number of fruit = 26.

    The probability of picking a pear = 5:26.

    The probability of picking an apple = 10:25.

    The probability of picking a pear and an apple = 5:26 * 10:25 = 50:650 = 1:13.

8. b)

The total number of fruit = 12.

The probability of picking a fig = 2;12.

The probability of picking an apple = 3;11.

The probability of picking a fig and an apple = 2;12 * 3;11 = 6;132 = .045.

Round up to .05.

9. d)

The overall rate for x workers = the number of toys/ the number of days, p/c. The number of toys one worker makes per day (rate) = p/cx. If q is the number of toys y workers make, and the rates are equal, then the number of toys made = the rate x.

The number of days * the number of workers gives us $q = p/cx \, (dy)$, so:

$q = pdy/cx$.

10. d)

The distance travelled = (35/1)(13) = 455 miles.

Chapter 5: Reading Review

Test Your Knowledge: Reading

Questions 1 – 4 are based on the following passage:

From *"On Lying Awake at Night"* **by Stewart Edward White** *(public domain)*:

About once in so often you are due to lie awake at night. Why this is so I have never been able to discover. It apparently comes from no predisposing uneasiness of indigestion, no rashness in the matter of too much tea or tobacco, no excitation of unusual incident or stimulating conversation. In fact, you turn in with the expectation of rather a good night's rest. Almost at once the little noises of the forest grow larger, blend in the hollow bigness of the first drowse; your thoughts drift idly back and forth between reality and dream; when—*snap!*—you are broad awake!

For, unlike mere insomnia, lying awake at night in the woods is pleasant. The eager, nervous straining for sleep gives way to a delicious indifference. You do not care. Your mind is cradled in an exquisite poppy-suspension of judgment and of thought. Impressions slip vaguely into your consciousness and as vaguely out again. Sometimes they stand stark and naked for your inspection; sometimes they lose themselves in the mist of half-sleep. Always they lay soft velvet fingers on the drowsy imagination, so that in their caressing you feel the vaster spaces from which they have come. Peaceful-brooding your *faculties* receive. Hearing, sight, smell—all are preternaturally keen to whatever of sound and sight and woods perfume is abroad through the night; and yet at the same time active appreciation dozes, so these things lie on it sweet and cloying like fallen rose-leaves.

Nothing is more fantastically unreal to tell about, nothing more concretely real to experience, than this undernote of the quick water. And when you do lie awake at night, it is always making its unobtrusive appeal. Gradually its hypnotic spell works. The distant chimes ring louder and nearer as you cross the borderland of sleep. And then outside the tent some little woods noise snaps the thread. An owl hoots, a whippoorwill cries, a twig cracks beneath the cautious prowl of some night creature—at once the yellow sunlit French meadows puff away—you are staring at the blurred image of the moon spraying through the texture of your tent.

(You have cast from you with the warm blanket the drowsiness of dreams. A coolness, physical and spiritual, bathes you from head to foot. All your senses are keyed to the last vibrations. You hear the littler night prowlers; you glimpse the greater. A faint, searching woods perfume of dampness greets your nostrils. And somehow, mysteriously, in a manner not to be understood, the forces of the world seem in suspense, as though a touch might crystallize infinite possibilities into infinite power and motion. But the touch lacks. The forces hover on the edge of action, unheeding the little noises. In all humbleness and awe, you are a dweller of the Silent Places.

The night wind from the river, or from the open spaces of the wilds, chills you after a time. You begin to think of your blankets. In a few moments you roll yourself in their soft wool. Instantly it is morning.

And, strange to say, you have not to pay by going through the day unrefreshed. You may feel like turning in at eight instead of nine, and you may fall asleep with unusual promptitude, but your journey will begin clear-headedly, proceed springily, and end with much in reserve. No languor, no dull headache, no exhaustion, follows your experience. For this once your two hours of sleep have been as effective as nine.

1. In Paragraph 2, "faculties" is used to mean:
    a) Teachers.
    b) Senses.
    c) Imaginations.
    d) Capacities.

2. The author's opinion of insomnia is that:
    a) It is not a problem because nights without sleep are refreshing.
    b) It can happen more often when sleeping in the woods because of the noises in nature.
    c) It is generally unpleasant, but sometimes can be hypnotic.
    d) It is the best way to cultivate imagination.

3. By "strange to say" in Paragraph 6, the author means:
    a) The experience of the night before had an unreal quality.
    b) The language used in describing the night before is not easily understood.
    c) It is not considered acceptable to express the opinion the author expresses.
    d) Contrary to expectations, one is well-rested after the night before.

4. How is this essay best characterized?
    a) A playful examination of a common medical problem.
    b) A curious look at both sides of an issue.
    c) A fanciful description of the author's experience.
    d) A horrific depiction of night hallucinations.

Questions 5-14 are based on the following passages:

Passage One
An excerpt from the essay "*Tradition and the Individual Talent*" by T.S. Eliot (public domain):

No poet, no artist of any art, has his complete meaning alone. His significance, his appreciation is the appreciation of his relation to the dead poets and artists. You cannot value him alone; you must set him, for contrast and comparison, among the dead. I mean this as a principle of aesthetic, not merely historical, criticism. The necessity that he shall conform, that he shall cohere, is not one-sided; what happens when a new work of art is created is something that happens simultaneously to all the works of art which preceded it. The existing monuments form an ideal order among themselves, which is modified by the introduction of the new (the really new) work of art among them. The existing order is complete before the new work arrives; for order to persist after the supervention of novelty, the *whole* existing order must be, if ever so slightly, altered; and so the relations, proportions, values of each work of art toward the whole are readjusted; and this is conformity between the old and the new. Whoever has approved this idea of order, of the form of European, of English literature, will not find it preposterous that the past should be altered by the present as much as the present is directed by the past. And the poet who is aware of this will be aware of great difficulties and responsibilities.

Passage Two
An excerpt from the Clive Bell's seminal art history book "*Art*" (public domain):

To criticize a work of art historically is to play the science-besotted fool. No more disastrous theory ever issued from the brain of a charlatan than that of evolution in art. Giotto[1] did not creep, a grub, that Titian[2] might flaunt, a butterfly. To think of a man's art as leading on to the art of someone else is to misunderstand it. To praise or abuse or be interested in a work of art because it leads or does not lead to another work of art is to treat it as though it were not a work of art. The connection of one work of art with another may have everything to do with history: it has nothing to do with appreciation. So soon as we begin to consider a work as anything else than an end in itself we leave the world of art. Though the development of painting from Giotto to Titian may be interesting historically, it cannot affect the value of any particular picture: aesthetically, it is of no consequence whatever. Every work of art must be judged on its own merits.

5. In Passage One, the word "cohere" is used to most closely mean:
   a) To be congruous with.
   b) To supplant.
   c) To imitate.
   d) To overhaul.
   e) To deviate from.

6. In Passage Two, the author alludes to a butterfly to contradict which concept?
   a) The theory of evolution is responsible for the discipline of art criticism.
   b) Scientific knowledge is not necessary to understand paintings.
   c) Artists who show off are doomed to be criticized.
   d) Art which finds inspiration in nature is the highest form of art.
   e) Titian's art is beautiful as a result of the horrible art that came before.

7. The author of Passage One would be most likely to support:
   a) An artist who imitated the great works of the past.
   b) An art critic who relied solely on evaluating the aesthetics of new art.
   c) A historian who studied the aesthetic evolution of art.
   d) An artist who was also a scientist.
   e) An artist who shouldered the burden of creating something new, while affecting the old, in the world of art.

8. The meaning of the sentence "To praise or abuse or be interested in a work of art because it leads or does not lead to another work of art is to treat it as though it were not a work of art" in Passage 2 means:
   a) Works of art cannot be judged primarily by their relation to one another.
   b) One should not vandalize works of art.
   c) It is necessary to understand how one work of art leads to another in order to judge it.
   d) Works of art must be treated with respect.
   e) Understanding works of art is reliant on seeing them on a historical scale.

---

[1] Giotto was an Italian painter during the Middle Ages.
[2] Titian was an Italian painter during the Renaissance.

9. The author of Passage One would likely agree with which of the following statements?
  a) The past is a monument that is unalterable by the present.
  b) Historical knowledge is entirely separate from artistic knowledge.
  c) To understand a novel written in the twentieth century, it is necessary to have some knowledge of nineteenth century literature.
  d) Painters of Italian descent are all related to one another.
  e) One cannot be a scholar of literary history without also being a scholar of scientific thought.

10. The authors of both passages would likely agree with which of the following statements?
  a) An aesthetic judgment is the greatest possible approach to art criticism.
  b) Knowledge of history compromises one's ability to criticize works of art.
  c) The painter Titian was able to create his art as a consequence of the art which came before his time.
  d) It is imperative to understand the progression from one work of art to another.
  e) Not all works of art are consequential.

Questions 11 and 12 are based on the following passage:

Excerpt from Anne Walker's "*A Matter of Proportion*," a short science-fiction story published in 1959 (public domain). In this excerpt, one character tells another about an injured man who is planning a secret operation:

On the way, he filled in background. Scott had been living out of the hospital in a small apartment, enjoying as much liberty as he could manage. He had equipment so he could stump around, and an antique car specially equipped. He wasn't complimentary about them. Orthopedic products had to be: unreliable, hard to service, unsightly, intricate, and uncomfortable. If they also squeaked and cut your clothes, fine!
Having to plan every move with an eye on weather and a dozen other factors, he developed an uncanny foresight. Yet he had to improvise at a moment's notice. With life a continuous high-wire act, he trained every surviving fiber to precision, dexterity, and tenacity. Finally, he avoided help. Not pride, self-preservation; the compulsively helpful have rarely the wit to ask before rushing in to knock you on your face, so he learned to bide his time till the horizon was clear of beaming simpletons. Also, he found an interest in how far he could go.

11. Why does Scott primarily avoid the help of others?
  a) He has found that he is usually better off without it.
  b) He does not want to rely on other people for anything.
  c) He is doing experiments to test his own limits.
  d) He is working on a secret operation and cannot risk discovery.
  e) He does not realize that he needs assistance.

12. "Orthopedic" in paragraph one most nearly means:
  a) Uncomfortable.
  b) Dangerous.
  c) Corrective.
  d) Enhanced.
  e) Complicated.

Questions 13 – 18 are based on the following passage:

Excerpt from Rennie W. Doane's *"Insects and Disease,"* a popular science account published in 1910 (public domain):

It has been estimated that there are about four thousand species or kinds of Protozoans, about twenty-five thousand species of Mollusks, about ten thousand species of birds, about three thousand five hundred species of mammals, and from two hundred thousand to one million species of insects, or from two to five times as many kinds of insects as all other animals combined.

Not only do the insects preponderate in number of species, but the number of individuals belonging to many of the species is absolutely beyond our comprehension. Try to count the number of little green aphis on a single infested rose-bush, or on a cabbage plant; guess at the number of mosquitoes issuing each day from a good breeding-pond; estimate the number of scale insects on a single square inch of a tree badly infested with San José scale; then try to think how many more bushes or trees or ponds may be breeding their millions just as these and you will only begin to comprehend the meaning of this statement.

As long as these myriads of insects keep, in what we are pleased to call their proper place, we care not for their numbers and think little of them except as some student points out some wonderful thing about their structure, life-history or adaptations. But since the dawn of history we find accounts to show that insects have not always kept to their proper sphere but have insisted at various times and in various ways in interfering with man's plans and wishes, and on account of their excessive numbers the results have often been most disastrous.

Insects cause an annual loss to the people of the United States of over $1,000,000,000. Grain fields are devastated; orchards and gardens are destroyed or seriously affected; forests are made waste places and in scores of other ways these little pests which do not keep in their proper places are exacting this tremendous tax from our people. These things have been known and recognized for centuries, and scores of volumes have been written about the insects and their ways and of methods of combating them.

Yellow fever, while not so widespread as malaria, is more fatal and therefore more terrorizing. Its presence and spread are due entirely to a single species of mosquito, *Stegomyia calopus*. While this species is usually restricted to tropical or semi-tropical regions it sometimes makes its appearance in places farther north, especially in summer time, where it may thrive for a time. The adult mosquito is black, conspicuously marked with white. The legs and abdomen are banded with white and on the thorax is a series of white lines which in well-preserved specimens distinctly resembles a lyre. These mosquitoes are essentially domestic insects, for they are very rarely found except in houses or in their immediate vicinity. Once they enter a room they will scarcely leave it except to lay their eggs in a near-by cistern, water-pot, or some other convenient place.

Their habit of biting in the daytime has gained for them the name of "day mosquitoes" to distinguish them from the night feeders. But they will bite at night as well as by day and many other species are not at all adverse to a daylight meal, if the opportunity offers, so this habit is not distinctive. The recognition of these facts has a distinct bearing in the methods adopted to prevent the spread of yellow fever. There are no striking characters or habits in the larval or pupal stages that would enable us to distinguish without careful examination this species from other similar forms with which it might be associated. For some time it was claimed that this species would breed only in clean water, but it has been found that it is not nearly so particular, some even claiming that it prefers foul water. I have seen them breeding in countless thousands in company with *Stegomyia scutellaris* and *Culex fatigans* in the sewer drains in Tahiti in the streets of Papeete. As the larva feed largely on bacteria one would expect to find them in exactly such places where the bacteria are of course abundant. The fact that they are able to live in any kind of water and in a very small amount of it well adapts them to their habits of living about dwellings.

13. Why does the author list the amounts of different species of organisms in paragraph 1?
   a) To illustrate the vast number of species in the world.
   b) To demonstrate authority on the subject of insects.
   c) To establish the relative importance of mollusks and birds.
   d) To demonstrate the proportion of insects to other organisms.

14. What does the author use "their proper place" at the beginning of paragraph 3?
   a) The author is alluding to people's tendency to view insects as largely irrelevant to their lives.
   b) The author feels that insects belong only outdoors.
   c) The author wants the reader to feel superior to insects.
   d) The author is warning that insects can evolve to affect the course of human events.

15. This passage can be characterized primarily as:
   a) Pedantic.
   b) Droll.
   c) Informative.
   d) Abstract.
   e) Cautionary.

16. The main idea of this passage is best summarized as:
   a) Disease-carrying mosquitoes have adapted to best live near human settlements.
   b) Insects can have a detrimental effect on the economy by destroying crops.
   c) Insects are numerous in both types of species and individuals within a species.
   d) Although people do not always consider insects consequential, they can have substantial effects on human populations.

17. The use of "domestic" in Paragraph 5 most nearly means:
   a) Originating in the United States.
   b) Under the care of and bred by humans.
   c) Fearful of the outdoors.
   d) Living near human homes.

18. Which of the following ideas would best belong in this passage?
   a) An historical example of the effect a yellow fever outbreak had on civilization.
   b) A biological explanation of how diseases are transmitted from insects to humans.
   c) A reference to the numbers of insects which live far away from human habitation.
   d) Strategies for the prevention of yellow fever and malaria.

Questions 19 – 26 are based on a long original passage (author Elissa Yeates):

The collapse of the arbitrage[3] firm Long-Term Capital Management (LTCM) in 1998 is explained by a host of different factors: its investments were based on a high level of leverage, for example, and it was significantly impacted by Russia's default on the ruble. However, sociologist Donald MacKenzie maintains that the main factor in LTCM's demise was that, like all arbitrage firms, it was subjected to the sociological phenomena of the arbitrage community; namely, imitation. Arbitrageurs, who are generally known to one another as members of a specific subset of the financial society, use decision-making strategies based not only on mathematical models or pure textbook reason, but also based upon their feelings and gut reactions toward the financial market and on the actions of their peers. This imitation strategy leads to the overlapping "super portfolio," which creates an inherent instability that leads to collapse, the most infamous example being LTCM.

The public opinion of the partners of the firm in 1998 was that it had acted cavalierly with borrowed capital. However, in actuality the firm's strategy was exceedingly conservative, with a diversified portfolio, overestimated risks, and carefully hedged investments. The firm even tested tactics for dealing with financial emergencies such as the collapse of the European Monetary Union. Before the 1998 crisis, those in LTCM were never accused of recklessness. Nor were they, as is sometimes explained, overly reliant on mathematical models. The statistical hubris explanation falters under MacKenzie's evidence that John Meriwether and the others who ran the firm made their investment decisions based more upon their intricate understandings of the arbitrage market rather than upon the pure results of mathematical analyses. The financial instability that was created was not the result of the decision-making of one firm; but rather, the collective patterns of decision-making of all of the arbitrage firms at the time.

The infamy of LTCM worked against the company. LTCM was composed of some of the most eminent minds in finance and it made devastating profits for the first few years that it was running. This led to imitation by other arbitrageurs who viewed the investments of LTCM as nearly sure bets. This type of replication of investment portfolios is not surprising, considering that arbitrageurs are all looking for similar types of pricing discrepancies and anomalies to exploit. The structure of arbitrageurs as a unique subset of the financial community who are largely personally known to one another further contributes to this phenomenon. Because of these factors over time the various players in the field of arbitrage created overlapping investments which MacKenzie dubs a "super portfolio." While LTCM alone may have created a geographically and industrially diverse portfolio, across the discipline of arbitrage as a whole capital flocked to similar investments.

Because of this super portfolio trend, multiple arbitrageurs were affected by the price changes of different assets caused by the actions of single independent firms. MacKenzie cites the example of the takeover of the investment bank Salomon Brothers by the Travelers Corporation. Salomon Brothers' portfolio, now under the management of someone who disliked the risks of arbitrage trading, liquidated its positions, which drove down the prices of assets in the markets in which it operated. The liquidation of the holdings of such a prominent player in the arbitrage game negatively affected the positions of every other firm that had a stake in those markets, including, of course, LTCM. This also illustrates the other sociological side of MacKenzie's argument: that arbitrageurs are subject to irrational internal pressures to cut their losses before their investments play out, which one of his interview subjects terms "queasiness" when faced with a stretch of losses.

---

[3] "Arbitrage" is a financial strategy which takes advantage of the temporary price differences of a single asset in different markets.

19. The second paragraph of this passage primarily aims to:
   a) Explain that recklessness with borrowed capital is never profitable.
   b) Explore the factors ultimately responsible for the demise of the arbitrage firm Long-Term Capital Management.
   c) Demonstrate how the practice of arbitrage works.
   d) Laud the use of statistical models in calculating financial risks.
   e) Present and dismiss several theories of the collapse of Long-Term Capital Management.

20. In paragraph 2, "devastating" is used to mean:
   a) Destructive.
   b) Attractive.
   c) Blasphemous.
   d) Considerable.
   e) Appalling.

21. The final paragraph in this passage:
   a) Refutes the argument presented in the second paragraph of the passage.
   b) Gives a logical example of the phenomenon described in the introductory first paragraph of the passage.
   c) Contains an ardent plea against the passage of arbitrage.
   d) Gives a step-by-step account of the demise of Long-Term Capital Management.
   e) Argues that an understanding of sociology is crucial to successful financial practice.

22. Which of the following is a best description of the author's approach to the topic?
   a) Impassioned exposition.
   b) Curious exploration.
   c) Gleeful detection.
   d) Disgusted condemnation.
   e) Serene indifference.

23. Which of the following most accurately summarizes the author's thesis?
   a) If Long-Term Capital Management had developed a superportfolio, it would not have collapsed.
   b) Financial markets are inherently instable because those who participate in them are subject to human faults.
   c) Arbitrage firms should always endeavor to have geographically and industrially diverse investments.
   d) Long-Term Capital Management collapsed because arbitrageurs across the industry were investing in the same things, which caused instability.
   e) Long-Term Capital Management was run by financiers who were reckless and overly dependent on mathematical models, which is why it collapsed.

24. "Hubris" in paragraph 2 most likely means:
   a) Mathematical model.
   b) Reliance.
   c) Arrogance.
   d) Denial.
   e) Mistake.

25. Which of the following facts would undermine the main argument of the passage?

    a) The European Monetary Union was close to collapse in 1998.

    b) Some arbitrage firms steered clear of the practice of superportfolios.

    c) The Travelers Corporation was run by financiers who favored the practice of arbitrage.

    d) Arbitrageurs rarely communicate with one another or get information from the same source.

    e) Mathematical models used in finance in the 1990s were highly reliable.

26. Which of the following supports the argument made in the third paragraph?

    a) A detailed outline of the statistical models used by Long-Term Capital Management to make decisions.

    b) An explanation of how other arbitrage firms were able to learn the tactics practiced by Long-Term Capital Management.

    c) Examples of the differences between different investment portfolios of arbitrage firms.

    d) An outline of sociological theories about decision-making processes.

    e) A map showing the geographical diversity of arbitrage investors.

Questions 26 – 27 are based on a long passage excerpted from Robert Louis Stevenson's classic novel Treasure Island (public domain). In this passage, the narrator tells about an old sailor staying at his family's inn.

He had taken me aside one day and promised me a silver fourpenny on the first of every month if I would only keep my "weather-eye open for a seafaring man with one leg" and let him know the moment he appeared. Often enough when the first of the month came round and I applied to him for my wage, he would only blow through his nose at me and stare me down, but before the week was out he was sure to think better of it, bring me my fourpenny piece, and repeat his orders to look out for "the seafaring man with one leg."

How that personage haunted my dreams, I need scarcely tell you. On stormy nights, when the wind shook the four corners of the house and the surf roared along the cove and up the cliffs, I would see him in a thousand forms, and with a thousand diabolical expressions. Now the leg would be cut off at the knee, now at the hip; now he was a monstrous kind of a creature who had never had but the one leg, and that in the middle of his body. To see him leap and run and pursue me over hedge and ditch was the worst of nightmares. And altogether I paid pretty dear for my monthly fourpenny piece, in the shape of these abominable fancies.

But though I was so terrified by the idea of the seafaring man with one leg, I was far less afraid of the captain himself than anybody else who knew him. There were nights when he took a deal more rum and water than his head would carry; and then he would sometimes sit and sing his wicked, old, wild sea-songs, minding nobody; but sometimes he would call for glasses round and force all the trembling company to listen to his stories or bear a chorus to his singing. Often I have heard the house shaking with "Yo-ho-ho, and a bottle of rum," all the neighbors joining in for dear life, with the fear of death upon them, and each singing louder than the other to avoid remark. For in these fits he was the most overriding companion ever known; he would slap his hand on the table for silence all round; he would fly up in a passion of anger at a question, or sometimes because none was put, and so he judged the company was not following his story. Nor would he allow anyone to leave the inn till he had drunk himself sleepy and reeled off to bed.

His stories were what frightened people worst of all. Dreadful stories they were—about hanging, and walking the plank, and storms at sea, and the Dry Tortugas, and wild deeds and places on the Spanish

Main. By his own account he must have lived his life among some of the wickedest men that God ever allowed upon the sea, and the language in which he told these stories shocked our plain country people almost as much as the crimes that he described. My father was always saying the inn would be ruined, for people would soon cease coming there to be tyrannized over and put down, and sent shivering to their beds; but I really believe his presence did us good. People were frightened at the time, but on looking back they rather liked it; it was a fine excitement in a quiet country life, and there was even a party of the younger men who pretended to admire him, calling him a "true sea-dog" and a "real old salt" and such like names, and saying there was the sort of man that made England terrible at sea.

In one way, indeed, he bade fair to ruin us, for he kept on staying week after week, and at last month after month, so that all the money had been long exhausted, and still my father never plucked up the heart to insist on having more. If ever he mentioned it, the captain blew through his nose so loudly that you might say he roared, and stared my poor father out of the room. I have seen him wringing his hands after such a rebuff, and I am sure the annoyance and the terror he lived in must have greatly hastened his early and unhappy death.

27. The purpose of Paragraph 3 is to:
   a) Illustrate how others view the captain.
   b) Explain the narrator's relationship with the captain.
   c) Give more background information about the inn where the narrator lives.
   d) Recount old seafaring lore.
   e) Explain why the captain is staying at this inn.

28. Which paragraph serves to evoke the life lived by sailors at sea?
   a) 1.
   b) 2.
   c) 3.
   d) 4.
   e) 5.

29. "Diabolical" in Paragraph 2 most nearly means:
   a) Angry.
   b) Judgmental.
   c) Contorted.
   d) Fiendish.
   e) Stoic.

30. What kind of character does the author reveal the captain to be the third paragraph?
   a) Temperamental.
   b) Generous.
   c) Jocund.
   d) Mysterious.
   e) Reserved.

31. What does the author reveal about the narrator in Paragraph 5?
   a) The narrator is afraid of the captain.
   b) The narrator is eager to go to sea.
   c) The narrator was often angry and annoyed.
   d) The narrator grew up in poverty.
   e) The narrator lost his father at an early age.

32. "Tyrannized" in Paragraph 4 is used to mean:
   a) Cajoled.
   b) Bullied.
   c) Frightened.
   d) Robbed.
   e) Ejected.

33. Which of the following statements about this passage is false?
   a) It is unclear whether the "seafaring man with one leg" actually exists.
   b) The narrator harbors a serious grudge against the captain.
   c) The narrator is interested in the captain's stories.
   d) The story takes place near the ocean.
   e) Most people who populate the story are afraid of the captain.

34. According to the captain, all of the following are hazards which can be encountered at sea EXCEPT:
   a) Hangings.
   b) Wicked men.
   c) Walking the plank.
   d) Storms.
   e) Sea monsters.

35. It can be inferred from the passage that:
   a) Singing was frowned upon in the community.
   b) The narrator never knew his mother.
   c) The narrator admired the captain.
   d) The captain is afraid of the seafaring man with one leg.
   e) The narrator went on to become a pirate.

36. By "they rather liked it" at the end of Paragraph 4, the author most closely means:
   a) The patrons of the inn enjoyed singing.
   b) The captain and others appreciated the rum available for sale at the inn.
   c) The narrator and his friends liked the stories the captain told.
   d) The captain provided entertainment at the inn, which would otherwise be boring.
   e) The narrator's parents liked having the captain around.

Questions 37 – 40 are based on a short passage excerpted from the introduction to The Best American Humorous Short Stories, edited by Alexander Jessup (public domain).

No book is duller than a book of jokes, for what is refreshing in small doses becomes nauseating when perused in large assignments. Humor in literature is at its best not when served merely by itself but when presented along with other ingredients of literary force in order to give a wide representation of life. Therefore "professional literary humorists," as they may be called, have not been much considered in making up this collection. In the history of American humor there are three names which stand out more prominently than all others before Mark Twain, who, however, also belongs to a wider classification: "Josh Billings" (Henry Wheeler Shaw, 1815-1885), "Petroleum V. Nasby" (David Ross Locke, 1833-1888), and "Artemus Ward" (Charles Farrar Browne, 1834-1867). In the history of American humor these names rank high; in the field of American literature and the American short story they do not rank so high. I have found nothing of theirs that was first-class both as humor and as short story. Perhaps just below these three should be mentioned George Horatio Derby (1823-1861), author of *Phoenixiana* (1855) and the *Squibob Papers* (1859), who wrote under the name "John Phoenix." As has been justly said, "Derby, Shaw, Locke and Browne carried to an extreme numerous tricks already invented by earlier American humorists, particularly the tricks of gigantic exaggeration and calm-faced mendacity, but they are plainly in the main channel of American humor, which had its origin in the first comments of settlers upon the conditions of the frontier, long drew its principal inspiration from the differences between that frontier and the more settled and compact regions of the country, and reached its highest development in Mark Twain, in his youth a child of the American frontier, admirer and imitator of Derby and Browne, and eventually a man of the world and one of its greatest humorists."

37. The author of this passage would disagree with all of the following statements EXCEPT:
    a) To be a successful storyteller, one must also be a professional literary humorist.
    b) Mark Twain is the most prominent American humorist.
    c) Lying with a straight face is a literary humorist device which had just been invented at the time this was published.
    d) The best joke books are the longest ones.
    e) Professional literary humorism is the highest form of writing.

38. The purpose of this passage is to:
    a) Scorn humorous writing as lesser than storytelling.
    b) Explain how writers use humorous literary devices.
    c) Provide contextual information about the landscape of American humorous writing.
    d) Make a case for the appreciation of the humorists Henry Shaw and David Locke.
    e) Deny the historical roots of American literary humor.

39. The word "prominently" in line four most closely means:
    a) Extravagantly.
    b) Inconspicuously.
    c) Significantly.
    d) Comically.
    e) Conceitedly.

40. Which of the following best summarizes the author's theory of the origins of American humorous writing?
    a) It started as a way of breaking away from British literary humor.
    b) It grew hand-in-hand with American storytelling.
    c) It was founded by Mark Twain.
    d) It was inspired by the differences between settlements and the frontier.
    e) It began with exaggerations and mendacity.

Test Your Knowledge: Reading – Answers

1. b)	21. b)
2. c)	22. b)
3. d)	23. d)
4. c)	24. c)
5. a)	25. d)
6. e)	26. b)
7. e)	27. a)
8. a)	28. d)
9. c)	29. d)
10. e)	30. a)
11. a)	31. e)
12. c)	32. b)
13. d)	33. b)
14. a)	34. e)
15. c)	35. c)
16. d)	36. d)
17. d)	37. b)
18. a)	38. c)
19. e)	39. c)
20. d)	40. d)

Chapter 7: The Writing Section Review

Test Your Knowledge: Multiple Choice

Questions 1 – 5 are based on the following original passage. Sentences are numbered at the end for easy reference within the questions.

Examining the impact my lifestyle has on the earth's resources is, I believe, a fascinating and valuable thing to do (1). According to the Earth Day Network ecological footprint calculator, it would take four planet earths to sustain the human population if everyone used as many resources as I do (2). My "ecological footprint," or the amount of productive area of the earth that is required to produce the resources I consume, is therefore larger than the footprints of most of the population (3). It is hard to balance the luxuries and opportunities I have available to me with doing what I know to be better from an ecological standpoint (4).

It is fairly easy for me to recycle, so I do it, but it would be much harder to forgo the opportunity to travel by plane or eat my favorite fruits that have been flown to the supermarket from a different country (5). Although I get ecological points for my recycling habits, my use of public transportation, and living in an apartment complex rather than a free-standing residence, <u>my footprint expands when it is taken into account my not-entirely-local diet</u>, my occasional use of a car, my three magazine subscriptions, and my history of flying more than ten hours a year (6). I feel that realizing just how unfair my share of the earth's resources have been should help me to change at least some of my bad habits (7).

1. Which of the following is the best version of sentence 1?
    a) It is fascinating and valuable to examine the impact that my lifestyle has on the earth's resources.
    b) Examining the impact my lifestyle has on the earth's resources is a fascinating and valuable thing to do.
    c) To examine the impact my lifestyle has on the earth's resources is fascinating and is also valuable.
    d) The impact of my lifestyle on the earth's resources is fascinating and valuable to examine.
    e) Examining the impact my lifestyle has on the earth's resources is, I believe, a fascinating and valuable thing to do.

2. How could sentences 2 and 3 best be combined?
   a) According to the Earth Day Network ecological footprint calculator, it would take four planet earths to sustain the human population if everyone used as many resources as I do because I have a very large "ecological footprint," which is the amount of productive area of the earth that is required to produce the resources I consume.
   b) According to the Earth Day Network ecological footprint calculator, which calculates the amount of productive area of the earth that is required to produce the resources one consumes, it would take four planet earths to sustain the human population if everyone had a footprint as large as mine.
   c) According to the Earth Day Network ecological footprint calculator, it would take four planet earths to sustain the human population if everyone used as many resources as I do; my "ecological footprint," or the amount of productive area of the earth that is required to produce the resources I consume, is therefore larger than the footprints of most of the population.
   d) According to the Earth Day Network ecological footprint calculator, which measures the amount of productive area of the earth that is required to produce the resources a person consumes, my footprint is larger than that of most; it would take four planet earths to sustain the human population if everyone consumed as much as I do.
   e) According to the Earth Day Network ecological footprint calculator, my "ecological footprint," or the amount of productive area of the earth that is required to produce the resources I consume, would require four planet earths if it were to be the footprint of the human population; it is therefore larger than the footprints of most of the population.

3. Sentence 4 would best fit if it were moved where in this composition?
   a) At the beginning of paragraph 2.
   b) After sentence 5.
   c) After sentence 6.
   d) At the end of paragraph 2.
   e) Sentence 4 is best left where it is.

4. Which two sentences would be improved by switching positions?
   a) 1 and 2.
   b) 3 and 4.
   c) 5 and 6.
   d) 6 and 7.
   e) 2 and 7.

5. Which of the following should replace the underlined portion of sentence 6?
   a) "my footprint expands when taken into account my not-entirely-local diet"
   b) "my footprint expands when taken into account are my not-entirely-local diet"
   c) "my footprint expands when we take into account my not-entirely-local diet"
   d) "my footprint expands when one takes into account my not-entirely-local diet"
   e) "my footprint expands when it is taken into account my not-entirely-local diet"

6. Which revision would most improve sentence 7?
   a) Eliminate the phrase "I feel that."
   b) Change "should help me" to "will help me."
   c) Add the phrase "In conclusion," to the beginning.
   d) Change "have been" to "has been."
   e) Eliminate the phrase "at least some of."

Questions 7 – 12 are based on the short passage below, which is excerpted from Thomas Huxley's preface to his Collected Essays: Volume V (public domain) and modified slightly. Sentences are numbered at the end for easy reference within the questions.

I had set out on a journey, with no other purpose than that of exploring a certain province of natural knowledge, I strayed no hair's breadth from the course which it was my right and my duty to pursue; and yet I found that, whatever route I took, before long, I came to a tall and formidable-looking fence (1). Confident I might be in the existence of an ancient and indefeasible right of way, before me stood the thorny barrier with its comminatory notice-board—"No Thoroughfare. By order" (2). There seemed no way over; nor did the prospect of creeping round, as I saw some do, attracts me (3). True there was no longer any cause to fear the spring guns and man-traps set by former lords of the manor; but one is apt to get very dirty going on all-fours (4). The only alternatives were either to give up my journey—which I was not minded to do—or to break the fence down and go through it (5). I swiftly ruled out crawling under as an option (6). I also ruled out turning back (7).

7. How could sentence 1 best be changed?
   a) The comma after journey should be removed.
   b) The comma after knowledge should be changed to a semicolon.
   c) "and yet" should be eliminated.
   d) Change "I had set out" to "I set out."
   c) No change.

8. Sentence 6 should be placed where in the passage?
   a) After sentence 1.
   b) After sentence 2.
   c) After sentence 3.
   d) After sentence 4.
   e) Left after sentence 5.

9. Which edit should be made in sentence 3?
   a) "nor" should be changed to "or."
   b) "seemed" should be changed to "seems."
   c) "me" should be changed to "I."
   d) "attracts" should be changed to "attract."
   e) No edit should be made.

10. How could sentences 6 and 7 best be combined?
   a) Swiftly, I ruled out crawling under as an option and also turning back.
   b) Ruling out two options swiftly: crawling under and turning back.
   c) I swiftly ruled out the options of crawling under or turning back.
   d) I ruled out crawling under as an option and I swiftly also ruled out turning back.
   e) I swiftly ruled out crawling under as an option and also turning back.

11. Which word could be inserted at the beginning of sentence 2 before "confident" to best clarify the meaning?
- a) Even.
- b) However.
- c) Hardly.
- d) Finally.
- e) Especially.

12. Which of the following is the best way to split sentence 1 into two separate sentences?
- a) I had set out on a journey, with no other purpose than that of exploring a certain province of natural knowledge. I strayed no hair's breadth from the course which it was my right and my duty to pursue; and yet I found that, whatever route I took, before long, I came to a tall and formidable-looking fence.

- b) I had set out on a journey, with no other purpose than that of exploring a certain province of natural knowledge, I strayed no hair's breadth from the course which it was my right and my duty to pursue. Yet I found that, whatever route I took, before long, I came to a tall and formidable-looking fence.

- c) I had set out on a journey, with no other purpose than that of exploring a certain province of natural knowledge, I strayed no hair's breadth from the course which it was my right and my duty to pursue; and yet I found that, whatever route I took, before long. I came to a tall and formidable-looking fence.

- d) I had set out on a journey. With no other purpose than that of exploring a certain province of natural knowledge, I strayed no hair's breadth from the course which it was my right and my duty to pursue; and yet I found that, whatever route I took, before long, I came to a tall and formidable-looking fence.

- e) I had set out on a journey, with no other purpose than that of exploring a certain province of natural knowledge, I strayed no hair's breadth from the course which it was my right and my duty to pursue; and yet. I found that, whatever route I took, before long, I came to a tall and formidable-looking fence.

Questions 13 – 27 are based on the short passage below:

[1]Sandra Cisneros, perhaps the best known Latina author in the United States, writes poems and stories whose titles alone – "Barbie-Q," "My Lucy Friend Who Smells Like Corn," "Woman Hollering Creek" – engage potential readers' curiosity. [2]Ironically, this renowned writer, whose books are printed on recycled paper, did not do wellin school. [3]When she lectures at schools and public libraries, Cisneros presents the evidence. [4]An elementary school report card containing Cs, Ds and a solitary B (for conduct). [5]Cisneros has a theory to explain her low grades: teachers had low expectations for Latina and Latino students from Chicago's South Side. [6]Despite the obstacles that she faced in school, Cisneros completed not only high school but also college. [7]Her persistence paid off in her twenties, when Cisneros was admitted <u>prestigious</u> to the Writers' Workshop at the University of Iowa.

[8]Cisneros <u>soon</u> observed that most of her classmates at the university seemed to have a common set of memories, based on middle-class childhoods, from which to draw in their writing. [9]Cisneros felt <u>decided</u> out of place. _____("9A")_____. [10]She decided to speak from her own experience. [11]Her voice, which by being one of a Latina living outside of the mainstream, found a large and attentive audience in 1984 with the publication of her first short story collection, The House on Mango Street. [12]<u>Today</u> the book is read by middle school, high school, and college students across the United States. [13]Cisneros uses her influence as a successful writer to help other Latina and Latino writers get their works published. [14]But <u>having made the argument that,</u> in order for large numbers of young Latinos to achieve literary success, the educational system itself must change. [15]Cisneros <u>hints</u> that she succeeded in spite of the educational system. "I'm the exception," she insists, "not the rule."

13. What change should be made to sentence 1?
    a) No Change.
    b) "author and writer."
    c) "author and novelist."
    d) "wordsmith and author."

14. What change should be made towards the end of sentence 1?
    a) No Change.
    b) "potential, reader's."
    c) "potential, readers."
    d) "potential readers."

15. What change should be made to sentence 2?
    a) No Change.
    b) "writer, who is recognized by her orange and black eyeglasses"
    c) "writer, who likes to write at night,"
    d) "writer"

16. What change should be made to sentence 3?
    a) No Change.
    b) "evidence: an"
    c) "evidence; an"
    d) "evidence an"

17. The best placement for the underlined portion in sentence 7 would be:
   a) Where it is now.
   b) Before the word admitted.
   c) Before the word "Writers'."
   d) Before the word "Workshop."

18. Which word would best replace the underlined portion in sentence 8?
   a) No Change.
   b) "furthermore"
   c) "nevertheless"
   d) "therefore"

19. Which of the following is the best beginning of sentence 9?
   a) No Change.
   b) "Cisneros herself,"
   c) "Cisneros, herself"
   d) "Cisneros,"

20. Which of the following is should replace the underlined word in sentence 9?
   a) No Change.
   b) "deciding"
   c) "decidedly"
   d) "decidedly and"

21. Which of the following true statements, if added at _____("9A")_____ , would best serve as a transition between the challenges Cisneros faced as an aspiring writer and her success in meeting those challenges?
   a) "She did not know what to do."
   b) "Then she had a break through."
   c) "At that point she almost went home to Chicago."
   d) "She wondered whether she was in the right field."

22. Which of the following changes should be made to sentence 11?
   a) No Change.
   b) "voice – that of a Latina living outside the mainstream –"
   c) "voice, being one of a Latina living outside the mainstream, it"
   d) "voice – in which it was a Latina living outside the mainstream –"

23. Which of the following changes should be made to sentence 11?
   a) No Change.
   b) "1984, With"
   c) "1984; with"
   d) "1984, with,"

24. Which of the following is the best change to the underlined word at the beginning of sentence 12?
   a) No Change.
   b) "In the future,"
   c) "Meanwhile,"
   d) "At the same time,"

25. Which of the following is the best replacement for the underlined portion in sentence 14?
   a) No Change.
   b) "she argues that,"
   c) "arguing that,"
   d) "she argues that, when"

26. Which choice best shows that Cisneros is emphatic about expressing the belief stated in the underlined portion of sentence 15?
   a) No Change.
   b) "Says."
   c) "Supposes."
   d) "Asserts."

27. The writer is considering deleting the last sentence. If the writer decided to delete this sentence, the paragraph would primarily lose a statement that:
   a) Enhances the subject and setting.
   b) Provides support for a point previously made.
   c) Humorously digresses from the main topic of the paragraph.
   d) Contradicts Cisneros's claim made earlier in the essay.

Questions 28-40 are based on the short passage below:

[1]Traveling on commercial airlines has changed substantially <u>over years</u>. [2]When commercial air travel first became available, it was so expensive that usually only businessmen could afford <u>to do so</u>. [3]Airplane efficiency, the relative cost of fossil fuels, <u>and using economies</u> of scale have all contributed to make travel by air more affordable and common. [4]These days, there are nearly 30,000 commercial air flights in the world each day!

[5]Depending on the size of the airport you are departing from, you should arrive 90 minutes to two and a half hours before your plane leaves. [6]Things like checking your luggage and flying internationally can make the process of getting to your gate take longer. [7]If you fly out of a very busy airport, like <u>LaGuardia, in</u> New York City, on a very busy travel day, like the day before Thanksgiving, you can easily miss your flight if you don't arrive early enough.

[8]Security processes for passengers have also changed. In the 1960s, there was <u>hardly any</u> security: you could just buy your ticket and walk on to the plane the day of the flight without even needing to show identification. [9]In the 1970s, American commercial airlines started installing sky marshals on many <u>flights, an</u> undercover law enforcement officers who would protect the passengers from a potential hijacking.

[10]Also in the early 1970s, the federal government began to require that airlines screen passengers and their luggage for things like weapons and bombs. [11]After the 2001 terrorist attacks in the United States, these requirements were <u>stringently enforced</u>. [12]Family members can no longer meet someone at the <u>gate; only ticketed passengers are allowed into the gate area</u>. [13]The definition of <u>weapons are</u> not allowed is expanded every time there is a new incident for example liquids are now restricted on planes after an attempted planned attack using gel explosives in 2006.

[14]Despite the hassles of traveling by air, it is still a boon to modern <u>life.</u> [14]<u>Still, some</u> businesses are moving away from sending employees on airplane trips, <u>as</u> face-to-face video conferencing technologies improve. [15]A trip which might take ten hours by car <u>can take only</u> two hours by plane. [16]However, the ability to travel quickly by air <u>will always be valued, by citizens</u> of our modern society.

28. Which of the following is the best change to the underlined portion of sentence 1?
- a) No Change.
- b) "over the years"
- c) "over time"
- d) Delete.

29. Which of the following is the best change to the underlined portion of sentence 2?
- a) No Change.
- b) "to do it"
- c) "to fly"
- d) "do so"

30. Which of the following is the best change to the underlined portion of sentence 3?
- a) No Change.
- b) "using economies"
- c) "and the use of economies"
- d) "and economies"

31. Which of the following is the best change to the underlined portion of sentence 7?
- a) No Change.
- b) "La Guardia in"
- c) "La Guardia; in"
- d) "La Guardia,"

32. Which of the following is the best change to the underlined portion of sentence 7?
- a) No Change.
- b) "hardly"
- c) "no"
- d) "barely'

33. Which of the following is the best change to the underlined portion of sentence 9?
- a) No Change.
- b) "flights; an"
- c) "flights. Marshals are"
- d) "flights, marshals are"

34. Which of the following is the best change to the underlined portion of sentence 11?
- a) No Change.
- b) "stiffly upheld"
- c) "enforced with more stringency"
- d) "more stringently enforced"

35. If the underlined portion in sentence 12 were deleted, the passage would lose:
  a) No Change.
  b) An explanation of the screening process.
  c) Ambiguity over why family members are no longer allowed at the gate.
  d) A further specific example of how regulations have changed over time.

36. Which of the following is the best change to the underlined portion in sentence 13?
  a) No Change.
  b) "weapon is"
  c) "weapons"
  d) "weapons which are"

37. Which of the following is the proper transition between sentences 13 & 14?
  a) No Change.
  b) "life. Some"
  c) "life even though some"
  d) "life, still some"

38. Which of the following is the best replacement for the underlined word in sentence 14?
  a) No Change.
  b) "because"
  c) "while"
  d) "since"

39. Which of the following is the best change to the underlined portion in sentence 15?
  a) No Change.
  b) "may only take"
  c) "takes only"
  d) "will only take"

40. Which of the following is the best change to the underlined portion in sentence 16?
  a) No Change.
  b) "citizens will always value"
  c) "will always, be valued by citizens"
  d) "will always be valued by citizens"

Test Your Knowledge: Multiple Choice – Answers

1. a)	21. b)
2. d)	22. b)
3. c)	23. a)
4. c)	24. a)
5. d)	25. b)
6. d)	26. d)
7. b)	27. b)
8. d)	28. b)
9. d)	29. c)
10. c)	30. c)
11. b)	31. b)
12. a)	32. a)
13. a)	33. c)
14. a)	34. d)
15. d)	35. d)
16. b)	36. d)
17. c)	37. c)
18. a)	38. a)
19. a)	39. b)
20. c)	40. d)

Test Your Knowledge: Essay

Prompt One
Provided below is an excerpt and a question. Use the excerpt to prompt your thinking, and then plan and write an essay in 25 minutes by answering the question from your perspective. Be sure to provide evidence.

- *General George S. Patton Jr. is quoted as having said, "No good decision was ever made in a swivel chair."*

Is it necessary to be directly in a situation in order to best understand what must be done?

Prompt Two
Provided below is an excerpt and a question. Use the excerpt to prompt your thinking, and then plan and write an essay in 25 minutes by answering the question from your perspective. Be sure to provide evidence.

- *In The Dispossessed, published in 1974, groundbreaking science fiction author Ursula K. LeGuin wrote, "You can't crush ideas by suppressing them. You can only crush them by ignoring them."*

Is it possible to get rid of an idea?

Prompt Three
Provided below is an excerpt and a question. Use the excerpt to prompt your thinking, and then plan and write an essay in 25 minutes by answering the question from your perspective. Be sure to provide evidence.

- *"The paradox of education is precisely this -- that as one begins to become conscious one begins to examine the society in which he is being educated." James Baldwin (1924-1987), American novelist, poet, and social critic*

Does a successful education require the examination of one's own society?

Test Your Knowledge: Essay – Answers

The following pages hold sample scored essays for topics one, two, and three. These are just examples - there are many ways that CASA essays can be scored high or low. Look for: reasoning, examples, word usage, coherency, and detail. There are no "right" answers on the CASA essay; the most important factor is that the argument be well developed.

Essays for Prompt One

Is it necessary to be directly in a situation to best understand what must be done?

Score of 5+:

General George Patton was speaking of war when he noted that "no good decision was ever made in a swivel chair;" however, that observation applies to situations beyond battle. While a big-picture perspective is useful in analyzing situations and deciding how to act, an on-the-ground outlook is essential. In matters of politics, and technology, to name two, the best-laid plans usually have to be changed to respond to changing circumstances.

One example which illustrates the necessity of on-the-ground action is the famous space flight of Apollo 13. Before launch, all plans were worked out to get the manned mission to the moon and back. However, due to a fluke set of circumstances – an oxygen tank explosion and the resulting technical problems – the plans had to change. The successful return of Apollo 13 and the survival of its crew would not have been possible without the quick thinking of the men on board. They first noticed the incident, well before the technical crew in Houston would have detected it from Earth. While the work of the technical crew was of course key as well, without the astronauts on board the ship to implement an emergency plan, the mission would surely have been lost.

Just as there are often unforeseen circumstances when implementing technology, politics can also be unpredictable. For example, the Cuban Missile Crisis in 1962 required immediate, on-the-ground decision making by the leaders of the United States. Prior to the Cold War standoff, President Kennedy and his advisors had already decided their hardline position against Soviet weapons expansion in the Western hemisphere. The Monroe Doctrine, status quo since the 1920s, held that European countries should not practice their influence in the Americas. The Soviet Union tested this line by establishing intermediate-range missiles on the island of Cuba. President Kennedy could not simply hold to the established wisdom, because the true limits had never been tested. Instead, to stave off the threat of attack, he was forced to act immediately as events unfolded to preserve the safety of American lives. The crisis unfolded minute-by-minute, with formerly confident advisors unsure of the smartest step. Eventually, after thirteen tense days, the leaders were able to reach a peaceful conclusion.

What these events of the 1960s illustrate is that the best laid plans are often rendered useless by an unfolding situation. For crises to be resolved, whether they be in war, technology, or politics; leaders must have level heads in the moment with up-to-date information. Therefore, plans established in advance by those in swivel chairs with level heads are not always the best plans to follow. History has shown us that we must be able to think on our feet as unforeseen situations unfold.

Score of 3-4:

It is often necessary to be directly on the ground as a situation unfolds to know what is best do to. This is because situations can be unpredictable and what you previously thought was the best course of action, is not always so. This can be seen in the unfolding events of the 1962 Cuban Missile Crisis.

The Cuban Missile Crisis happened in 1962, during the presidency of John F. Kennedy, when Nikita Khrushchev, president of the Soviet Union, developed an intermediate-range missile base on the island of Cuba, within range of the United States. Since the Monroe Doctrine in the 1920s, the United States leaders have declared that they would not tolerate this kind of aggression. However, the decisions that had been made by leaders in the past, removed from the situation, were no longer relevant. It was necessary for President Kennedy to make decisions as events unfolded.

As the Cuban Missile Crisis shows us, at turning points in history decisions have to be made as events unfold by those who are in the middle of a situation. Otherwise, we would all be acting according to what those in the past and those removed from the challenge thought was best. Following the Monroe Doctrine could have resulted in unnecessary violence.

Score of 2 or Less:

It is necessary to make decisions while in the middle of a situation, not above the situation, because there is always information that is only known to people in the middle of the situation. For example, in a war, the strategists in Washington might have an overall aim in the war, but they would be unable to know what it best to do on the ground. Situations like running out of ammunition or the enemy having an unexpected backup could change the decisions that need to be made. This was especially true before cell phones and other digital technologies made communication easier.

Essays for Prompt Two

Is it possible to get rid of an idea?

Score of 5+:

The suppression of ideas has been attempted over and over throughout history by different oppressive regimes. This theme has been explored as well in literature, through such dystopian works as 1984 and Fahrenheit 451. But these histories and stories always play out the same way: eventually, the repressed idea bubbles to the surface and triumphs. Ursula K. LeGuin acknowledged this by saying that ideas can be crushed not by suppression, but by omission.

In Aldous Huxley's novel Brave New World, the world government maintains order not by governing people strictly and policing their ideas, but by distracting them. Consumption is the highest value of the society. When an outsider to the society comes in and questions it, he is exiled – not to punish him, but to remove his influence from society. The government of the dystopia has learned that the best way to maintain control is to keep citizens unaware of other, outside ideas. This theme resonates with a modern audience more than other, more authoritarian tales of dystopia because in our society, we are less controlled than we are influenced and persuaded.

Repressing ideas through harsh authoritarian rule has proven time and again to be ultimately fruitless. For example, in Soviet Russia during the 1920s and 1930s, Josef Stalin attempted to purge his society of all religious belief. This was done through suppression: discriminatory laws were enacted, members of the clergy were executed, and the religious citizenry were terrified. While these measures drastically crippled religious institutions, they were ineffective at completely eliminating the idea of religion. Beliefs and traditions were passed down in communities clandestinely throughout the repressive rule of Stalin. After the fall of the Soviet Union, it became clear that religion had survived all along.

We see throughout literature and history that ignoring ideas and distracting people from them is generally more effective than to attempt to stamp an idea out through means of suppression. Authoritarian rule, in fact, can do the opposite: by dramatizing and calling attention to an idea in the name of condemning it, a regime might actually strengthen that idea.

Score of 3-4:

We have seen different governments try to crush out ideas throughout history. However, they are never actually successful in doing so. An idea can be ignored or suppressed, but it will never really go away. This is illustrated in the survival of religion in the Soviet Union.

In Soviet Russia during the 1920s and 1930s, Josef Stalin attempted to purge the society of all religious belief. This was done through suppression: discriminatory laws, execution of the clergy, and use of terror. While this harmed religious institutions, they were ineffective at crushing the idea of religion. Beliefs and traditions were passed down in communities secretly throughout the rule of Stalin. After the fall of the Soviet Union, it became clear that religion had survived all along.

The same kind of thing happened with apartheid law in South Africa. Even though there were laws against black Africans and white Africans using the same facilities, the idea caught fire, especially because of an international outcry against the law.

We see throughout history that suppressing ideas does not crush them. Authoritarian rule, in fact, can do the opposite: by calling attention to an idea in the name of condemning it, a regime might actually strengthen that idea.

Score of 2 or Less:

It is not possible to crush out an idea by ignoring it or by suppressing it. All throughout history, whenever anyone has tried to do this, they might be temporarily successful but the idea will always survive or come back. For example in the Soviet Union religion was suppressed. People were not allowed to practice their religion. But after the government fell, religion still existed – people had held on to their ideas during the time of suppression.

Essays for Prompt Three

Does a successful education require the examination of one's own society?

Score of 5+:

James Baldwin noted that education is a paradox – as one becomes educated, one starts to question the educators. This is necessarily true, because an education is not just a mastery of facts and information but also acquiring the ability to think critically and forge new connections. Progress in society comes from people who understand the thought that came before and are then able to take it one step further. This theme plays out in social activism and in science, for example.

A society's understanding of human rights is constantly evolving. For this process to continue, each generation must question the mores taught by the previous generation. This process can be seen in America in the progression of women's rights, the rights of non-whites, religious rights, and the rights of the disabled. One hundred years ago, these groups had far less constitutional protection than they do today. It takes groups of educated people with a forward-thinking understanding to advocate and press for changes to be made. To take one example, women have gone from not having the right to vote in 1912 to, one hundred years later, women beginning to run for the highest political office. This happened because people like Elizabeth Cady Stanton, a suffragist in the 1850s, and Marsha Griffiths, the Representative in Congress in the 1970s who championed for the Equal Rights Amendment, were able to take the precepts of justice and equality taught to them and take them a step further by applying them to women's rights.

This pattern of taking knowledge a step further can also be seen in the fields of science and mathematics. Sir Isaac Newton, one of the inventors of calculus, is attributed with saying he "stood on the shoulders of giants." He took the concepts well established in mathematics – geometry and algebra – and used the tools in a new way to create calculus. To do this, he had to both already understand what was known in the field but also be able to look at it critically. Without people doing this, fields like science and math would never progress.

A society that is interested in advancing, in rights, science, and every other field, must educate its citizens not to only understand the knowledge of the past but also to criticize prior thought and look at things in a new way. This is what James Baldwin meant – a truly educated person will question everything, even his or her own society, in order to progress.

Score of 3-4:

James Baldwin noted that education is a paradox – as one becomes educated, one starts to question the educators. This is true because an education is not just a mastery of facts and information but also ability to think critically and forge new connections. Progress in society comes from people who understand the thought that came before and are then able to take it one step further. One example of this is in human and political rights.

A society's understanding of human rights is constantly evolving. For this process to continue, each generation must question the mores taught by the previous generation. This process can be seen in America in the progression of women's rights, the rights of non-whites, religious rights, and the rights of the disabled. One hundred years ago, these groups had far less constitutional protection than they do today. It takes groups of educated people with a forward-thinking understanding to press for changes to be made. To take one example, women have gone from not having the right to vote in 1912 to, one hundred years later, women beginning to run for the highest political office. This happened because people like Elizabeth Cady Stanton, a suffragist in the 1850s, and Marsha Griffiths, the Representative in Congress in the 1970s who championed for the Equal Rights Amendment, were able to take the precepts of justice and equality taught to them and take them a step further by applying them to women's rights.

A society that is interested in advancing, in rights every other field, must educate its citizens not to only understand the knowledge of the past but also to criticize prior thought and look at things in a new way. This is what James Baldwin meant – a truly educated person will question everything, even his or her own society, in order to progress.

Score of 2 or Less:

James Baldwin said that education is a paradox – as one becomes educated, one starts to question the educators. He is right about this, because being educated is not just about knowing the facts. It is also about critical thinking. Without thinking critically about one's own society, then people never make progress. This was necessary for things like civil rights, they could not just accept what was taught in the schools about the rights people should have. Probably the most important part of being educated is questioning the society you live in.

31247488R00073

Made in the USA
Lexington, KY
03 April 2014